450

D1017391

THE WOMAN'S DAY
Chicken Cookbook

EDITED BY *Carol Truax*

Simon and Schuster
New York

Contents

6   Contents

Introduction

"Chicken every Sunday" and "A chicken in every pot" are two of our American slogans which show how closely we have always associated poultry with prosperity. Once expensive, it is no longer the luxury it used to be, for the prices of other meats have soared so high that the least expensive of fine foods is fowl. In addition to being good to your budget, it tastes good and is good for you, as it is low in calories and cholesterol while high in protein, iron, riboflavin and niacin. Pennywise housewives are wise to chicken!

Birds can be beautiful, whether cooked by someone who can scarcely boil water or by a chef of the Cordon Bleu; the former can thrust a roaster into the oven and ignore it until the timer goes off, while the latter may wish to bone some chicken breasts, brown them in clarified butter with crushed garlic, simmer them in white wine, ignite some warmed brandy over them, and blanket them in a sauce made of egg yolks, heavy cream and more brandy. For those of us who want something in between, there are countless nice-and-simple and nice-and-fancy recipes to choose from. In fact, here are 365 of them in case you want chicken every day of the week as well as Always on Sunday. And if there are any leftovers (accidental or intentional), many of the recipes are just as good if they are made with chicken that has been previously cooked. All recipes made with previously cooked chicken are marked with an asterisk (*).

BUYING

Who ever heard of a double-breasted broiler or a four-legged fryer? They're no surprise to shoppers in our modern markets, where packages are available containing anything from whole chickens to drumsticks to backs and necks for soup. Since sections are more expensive than an entire bird, and cut-up chickens cost a little more than the ones you dismember yourself, you can save money by doing it yourself. Cutting up chicken is easy.

Boning isn't difficult, either, if you have a thin-bladed sharp knife or kitchen scissors. Don't worry about the appearance of the boned pieces, as they will return to their original shape as they cook.

Poultry has changed for the better in many ways. Broilers are no longer scrawny, the white meat on large roasters is not apt to be dry and the dark strong in flavor, and the chore of removing pinfeathers with eyebrow tweezers is a thing of the past. It is true that most meats come packaged, so that we are not able to handle and inspect chickens the way our mothers used to do, but the government is very careful about giving out its label stating that the chicken has been "Inspected for Wholesomeness by the United States Department of Agriculture." Be sure to check for this, and for the seal saying "Grade A," which is worn by the poultry in most good markets.

You need from 12 ounces to a pound of poultry per serving. Two pounds of the meatier sections, such as the breast, is the equivalent of 3 to 3½ pounds of whole chicken. Large chickens are meatier than small ones.

After making your purchase, open the package before putting it in the refrigerator. Either then, or before cooking, rinse meat quickly in cold water and pat dry; never soak poultry in water.

Broiler-fryers are the children of the poultry world, aged from 8 to 12 weeks and weighing from 1½ to 3½ pounds. They are not only good for broiling and frying but, despite their names, are also good when roasted.

Roasters are adolescents, ranging from 12 weeks to 4 months in age. They weigh from 3½ to 6 pounds, are plumper than the young fry, and contain more fat; their bodies are more compact. They may be potted or stewed as well as roasted.

Fowl are the senior citizens, and have several advantages: they are apt to be less expensive and, in addition to fricasseeing and braising, they are excellent for dishes requiring a quantity of cooked meat. They also yield a good supply of chicken broth, and fat for baking and sautéeing.

Cornish game hens are a cross between Plymouth Rock chickens and game hens. Weighing from 1 to 2 pounds, the smaller ones each make an individual serving and the larger ones may be cut in half to serve two.

Capons, the kings of chicken, are desexed males, with a good supply of tender meat. They are expensive, weigh from 6 to 9 pounds, and are fine for roasting.

HERBS AND SPICES

Herbs and chicken go together like a horse and carriage, providing an almost infinite variety of flavors to suit individual tastes. Many recipes in this book list a specific herb, but that need not limit you, since herbs and spices are not absolutes in most recipes. If, for example, you dislike even the faintest trace of licorice, use chives where tarragon is suggested, and if you dislike chili, simply omit it. Also, if no herb or spice is suggested, feel free to improvise.

Fresh herbs are obviously the best, but frozen or dried are sat-isfactory. When using fresh herbs, use about three times as much as dried. Many herbs can be grown in almost any climate, and take little space in the garden. Some will grow in window boxes and even in pots.

Don't buy large quantities of dried herbs and spices, as many tend to lose flavor with age. Buying a blend of herbs from a rep-utable herb farm is wise: they know more than most of us do about blending them. *Fines herbes* is usually a blend of parsley, chervil and chives, with basil or thyme sometimes replacing the chervil. "Poultry seasoning" is another excellent and very useful blend.

Avoid using the same herbs and spices too often—experiment! And don't overseason; you can always add more to taste but you can't remove it.

There are many ways of using herbs and spices. For example, rub some on a roasting chicken while salting it, put some in its cavity instead of stuffing, or use them in the stuffing itself. It isn't difficult to insert tarragon under the skin of a chicken: sim-ply make a small slit in the skin of breasts and thighs, thrust in a finger to loosen it from the flesh, and poke fresh tarragon into the space. Bay leaf and garlic can add zest to stews and fricassees, and there are many ways of enhancing and varying the flavor of gravy.

Although they do not, strictly speaking, belong in this category, lemon and onions are some of the best flavorings for chicken.

HERBS AND SPICES WITH AN AFFINITY FOR POULTRY

basil	garlic	rosemary
bay leaf	ginger	sage
chervil	oregano	savory
chili	paprika	tarragon
chives	parsley	winter savory
cloves	pepper (*freshly ground*	
curry	is recommended as its	
dill	flavor is far superior)	

PART I

Recipes by Technique

1 *Roasting*

After removing the giblets and neck, which are usually inside the body cavity, wipe the chicken with a damp cloth and sprinkle it with a little salt inside and outside. If you wish to stuff the chicken, the stuffing should be added just before roasting. Approximately 1 cup of stuffing for each 2 pounds of poultry is a basic rule. Pack the stuffing *lightly* into the body and neck cavities, filling them about ¾ full, since stuffing expands. Fasten the cavities with poultry pins or sew them shut. Fold the wing tips under the back and tie the legs together close to the body. Place in a roaster or an open pan in a preheated oven at 350°. Baste if you wish (it is not essential) with butter or margarine, vegetable oil, broth, wine or pan drippings. Broiler-fryers, weighing from 2½ to 3½ pounds, will take about 1¼ hours (190° on a thermometer) and roasters weighing from 4½ to 7 pounds will take from 2 to 3 hours. Game hens, weighing 1 to 1½ pounds, take 45 minutes. If the bird is getting too brown, cover it loosely with foil.

Roasted chicken takes kindly to gravy, which is not hard to make. Remove the bird from the pan and keep it warm. Pour the drippings into a bowl or measuring cup and let stand until the fat rises to the top. This can be speeded up by putting it in the refrigerator or freezing compartment. Skim off most of the fat and return drippings to pan. For 2 cups of gravy, add 3 tablespoons of flour to about 3 or 4 tablespoons of drippings; stir until blended. Add 1½ to 2 cups of liquid (water, wine or broth) and boil, stirring, for several minutes, to desired consistency. Season to taste.

Carving Poultry

It is easier if, as you carve, you put the pieces onto a separate plate, unless you have a very large platter.

1. Cut the legs from the bird following the contour of the body. Sever the joint between drumstick and thigh. Carve meat from the thigh and, when carving a turkey, carve slices also from the drumstick.

2. Cut off the wings, sever the joint on large birds.

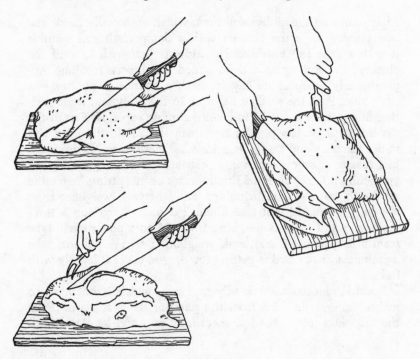

3. Carve the breast by cutting thin slices parallel to the breast starting about halfway up and then starting each slice a little higher up in the breast.

Don't carve more than you think you will need.

For serving duck, it is easiest to cut them in quarters with poultry shears. Game hens are also best served by cutting in half with shears.

Roast Chicken

1 roasting chicken, 4 to 5 pounds
1 to 1½ teaspoons salt
¼ teaspoon pepper
2 tablespoons melted butter *and/or* 2 teaspoons
    lemon juice

Rinse the chicken and pat dry. Sprinkle inside and out with salt and pepper. (You need not sprinkle the inside of the roaster if it is to be stuffed. In that case, 1 teaspoon of salt is enough.) Rub outside with butter and/or lemon juice. Truss the bird by folding the wings under the back and tying the drumsticks together close to the body. Fill the body and neck cavities about ¾ full with the stuffing of your choice and truss after stuffing. Stuff only a short time before roasting. Brush with butter and/or lemon juice and bake at 350° for about 1¼ hours or until tender. Baste with pan juices. Add a little broth to baste with if necessary. Make gravy (see page 15). Makes 4 to 6 servings.

Stuffed Roast Capon

> 1 capon, about 6 pounds
> Salt and pepper to taste
> 3 to 4 cups stuffing (favorite recipe or mix)
> 2 tablespoons butter *or* margarine, melted
> Juice of 1 lemon
> 2 tablespoons flour blended with 3 tablespoons water
> 1½ cups chicken broth

Season capon inside and out with salt and pepper. Stuff neck and body cavities; truss. Put on rack in shallow pan, brush with 1 teaspoon butter and the lemon juice. Insert meat thermometer. Roast at 325°, basting often with butter or pan drippings, 3½ hours or until leg is very soft when pressed between fingers. Remove capon to carving board. To make gravy, stir flour mixture into pan drippings, scraping up brown particles. Stir in 1½ cups broth gradually and cook and stir until thickened and smooth. Add salt and pepper. Makes about 2 cups gravy. Serve carved capon with stuffing and gravy. Makes 8 servings.

Roast Cornish Hens

> 4 game hens, about 1 pound *each*
> 1 teaspoon salt
> 4 slices bacon
> ¼ cup butter
> ½ cup chicken broth
> ½ cup heavy cream
> 1 teaspoon cornstarch *or* 1 tablespoon flour
> Juice and grated rind of 1 lemon

Sprinkle the game hens inside and out with salt and wrap each in a piece of bacon. (Fill the hens about ⅘ full with stuffing, if you wish.) Brown in butter in a casserole or heavy pot. Bake at 350°, uncovered, for half an hour, basting with butter and drippings in the pot. Combine the broth and cream and pour over; bake for another 20 to 30 minutes until tender. Remove hens and keep warm. Thicken sauce slightly with a paste made from cornstarch or flour and water and simmer 5 minutes. Add lemon juice and sprinkle with rind. Pour over hens and serve at once. Or if you prefer, serve sauce separately. Makes 4 servings.

Foil-Roasted Chicken

        2 whole broiler-fryers, 2 to 3 pounds *each*
        1 green pepper, cut in rings
        3 onions, halved
        6 small potatoes, halved
        4 carrots and 2 celery stalks, cut diagonally in 1" pieces
        1 can (14½ ounces) tomatoes
          Salt and pepper to taste
        2 tablespoons margarine, melted
          Paprika

In large piece of foil in roasting pan, arrange chickens and vegetables, except tomatoes. Empty can of tomatoes over all and season with salt and pepper. Wrap foil loosely around chickens and secure edges to keep moisture in. Roast at 375° for 1 hour, or until vegetables are tender. Turn back foil and baste chickens with pan juices. Brush with margarine and sprinkle with paprika. Continue roasting 20 minutes, or until chickens are tender and browned. Makes 6 servings.

Pot-Roasted Chicken with Vegetables

Stuffing (see below)
1 roasting chicken, 3½ to 4 pounds
Vegetable oil
Salt and pepper
4 medium potatoes, peeled
4 carrots, cut in chunks
4 small white onions

Stuff chicken and sew or skewer openings. Tie legs together and brown chicken on all sides in small amount of oil in heavy kettle or Dutch oven. Put chicken on rack in kettle. Season with salt and pepper and add ¾ cup water. Cover and simmer 1 hour. Add vegetables and season. Simmer, covered, 20 minutes longer. Makes 4 servings.

Stuffing

1½ cups chopped celery and leaves
1½ cups chopped onion
1 teaspoon poultry seasoning
¾ teaspoon salt
⅛ teaspoon pepper
3 tablespoons margarine
⅓ cup water
2 cups soft stale bread crumbs

Cook celery, onion, poultry seasoning, salt and pepper in margarine until vegetables are limp but not brown. Add water and bread crumbs; mix well.

Roast Chicken with Rice Stuffing

3 tablespoons butter *or* margarine
1 rib celery and top, chopped
1 small onion, chopped
4 cups cooked brown or white rice
  Grated rind and juice of 1 lemon
1 teaspoon marjoram
½ teaspoon thyme
1 whole broiler-fryer (about 3½ pounds)
  Salt and pepper to taste

To make stuffing, melt 2 tablespoons butter in skillet over medium heat and sauté celery and onion until crisp-tender. Stir in rice, lemon peel (reserve juice), marjoram and thyme. Spoon lightly into neck and body cavities of chicken. Close openings with poultry pins. (Bake any extra stuffing alongside chicken.) Brush chicken with remaining 1 tablespoon butter, melted, and the lemon juice; season with salt and pepper. Bake in 400° oven about 1 hour and 20 minutes, or until chicken is tender and browned. Makes 4 to 6 servings.

Roast Chicken with Brown-Rice Stuffing

1 chicken, 3 to 4 pounds
3 tablespoons margarine
1 cup chopped celery
½ cup chopped onion
3 cups water
1 cup raw brown rice
1 teaspoon salt
½ teaspoon marjoram
2 tablespoons lemon juice
  Seasoned salt

Mince giblets and sauté in 2 tablespoons margarine in large saucepan. Add celery and onion and sauté until golden. Add water and bring to boil, then stir in rice, salt and marjoram. Cover and simmer 25 minutes, or until liquid is absorbed; cool. Stuff chicken with rice mixture and truss. Brush with remaining margarine, softened, and the lemon juice. Sprinkle with seasoned salt. Roast, basting occasionally, in preheated 350° oven 1½ hours, until well browned and tender. Makes 4 servings.

Roast Chicken with Pecan-Rice Stuffing

> 1 roasting chicken, about 4½ pounds
> Salt and pepper
> 1 cup *each* chopped onion and celery
> 1 tablespoon butter *or* margarine
> ½ cup coarsely chopped pecans
> 3 cups cooked rice
> 1 tablespoon *each* thyme and marjoram
> 2 tablespoons flour blended with 3 tablespoons water
> 1½ cups chicken broth

Rub chicken inside and out with salt and pepper to taste. In skillet sauté onion and celery in butter until tender. Add pecans and sauté a few minutes; toss with rice, thyme, marjoram and 1 teaspoon salt; stuff in neck and body cavities; truss. (Bake any extra stuffing in casserole or foil along with chicken.) Roast on rack at 350°, basting frequently with pan juices, 1 hour and 45 minutes, or until leg is very soft when pressed between fingers and thermometer registers 185°. Remove to carving board. To make gravy, stir flour mixture into pan drippings, scraping up brown particles. Gradually stir in broth and cook and stir until thickened and smooth. Adjust seasonings. Makes about 2 cups gravy. Carve chicken and serve with stuffing and gravy. Makes 6 servings.

Rice-Stuffed Rock Cornish Hens

    4 small or 2 larger hens
    Juice of 1 lemon
    1 teaspoon salt
    ¼ teaspoon pepper
    3 slices bacon, diced
    ¼ pound mushrooms, sliced
    2 scallions, chopped fine
    ¾ cup cooked rice
    ¼ cup chicken broth
    ¼ cup sherry
    Melted butter

Rub hens inside and out with lemon juice, salt and pepper. Sauté the bacon and remove pieces. Sauté the mushrooms in bacon drippings, add scallions and sauté 3 minutes. Mix in the rice, broth, and sherry. Add bacon pieces, mix well, and stuff the hens. Brush with melted butter and bake, uncovered, at 350° for 45 minutes. Baste several times with pan juices, adding a little hot water and butter if needed. Pour juices over the birds. Makes 4 servings.

Pot-Roasted Chicken Stuffed with Vegetables

    1 roasting chicken, 4 to 5 pounds
    Homemade or packaged stuffing
    Vegetable oil
    Salt and pepper
    ¾ cup water
    6 medium potatoes, peeled
    4 carrots, cut in chunks
    6 small white onions
    ¼ pound whole green beans
    1 package (10 ounces) Fordhook lima beans

Fill chicken with stuffing and truss. Tie legs together and brown on all sides in small amount of oil in heavy kettle. Pour off fat and put chicken on rack in kettle. Season with salt and pepper and add water. Bring to boil, cover and simmer 1 hour. Add vegetables and season. Simmer, covered, ½ hour longer, or until chicken and vegetables are tender. Makes 6 servings.

Bread Stuffing

> 1 medium onion, minced
> 6 tablespoons butter
> 2 cups soft bread crumbs *or* 3 cups stale bread cut into ¼" cubes
> 1 teaspoon salt
> ½ teaspoon thyme
> ½ teaspoon savory
> ½ teaspoon tarragon
> ¼ teaspoon pepper
> 2 tablespoons sherry *or* lemon juice

Sauté the onion in 3 tablespoons butter until tender but not brown. Mix into the bread and add the remaining butter, melted, and remaining ingredients. Toss well and taste for salt.

Cornbread Stuffing

> ½ pound bulk pork sausage
> 2 tablespoons water
> 1 medium onion, chopped fine
> 1 cup finely diced celery
> 1 teaspoon poultry seasoning
> 1 teaspoon salt
> 3 cups crumbled cornbread *or* cornbread crumbs

Cook the sausage with water over low heat, breaking it up and stirring with a fork. Remove meat and set aside. Brown the onion and celery lightly in the fat; add poultry seasoning and salt. Mix with the cornbread and sausage.

Sausage Stuffing

   ¼ pound sausage meat
   2 tablespoons butter
   2 tablespoons minced onion
   ½ teaspoon salt
   ¼ teaspoon pepper
   ¼ cup chopped parsley
   3 cups soft stale bread crumbs *or* 4 cups cubed
      stale bread
    Milk

Sauté the sausage meat, breaking it up and stirring with a fork. Add butter, onion, salt and pepper and cook 3 minutes. Add parsley and bread, toss, and add milk just to moisten.

Rice Stuffing with Chicken Livers

   4 to 6 chicken livers
   ¼ cup butter
   ¼ cup minced onion
   ½ cup minced celery
   2 tablespoons minced parsley
   1 cup raw rice
   1 teaspoon salt
   1 teaspoon poultry seasoning
   ⅛ teaspoon thyme
  1½ cups water

Sauté the livers in 2 tablespoons butter, remove and chop. Add remaining butter to the pan and sauté the onion, celery, and parsley for 2 minutes. Add the rice, seasonings, and water. Return chicken livers to the pan and cook gently and stir for a few minutes. The rice should not be completely cooked.

Ham Stuffing

> 2 medium onions, chopped
> ¼ pound boiled ham, chopped
> 2 tablespoons butter
> 2 cups toasted bread crumbs *or* croutons
> ½ teaspoon salt
> ½ teaspoon poultry seasoning
> ¼ teaspoon pepper
> 1 tablespoon brandy

Sauté the onions and ham in butter. Add the remaining ingredients and toss.

Nut Stuffing

> 2 medium onions, chopped
> 2 tablespoons minced parsley
> ¼ cup butter *or* margarine
> ½ teaspoon poultry seasoning *or* ¼ teaspoon *each* of thyme and sage
> 1 teaspoon salt
> ½ teaspoon pepper
> 1½ to 3 cups soft bread crumbs
> ½ cup chopped pecans

Sauté the onion and parsley in butter or margarine until onion is soft but not brown. Add remaining ingredients and heat and stir until well mixed. The amount of bread depends on the size of the bird. A 2½- to 3-pound chicken takes 1½ cups, a 5-pound bird 3 cups.

Wheat Pilaf Stuffing

⅓ cup minced scallions
¼ cup butter
1½ cups cracked wheat
3 cups chicken broth
1 teaspoon thyme
½ teaspoon sage
1 teaspoon salt
¼ teaspoon pepper
1 cup peeled diced apple

Sauté the scallions in butter for 2 or 3 minutes. Add the wheat and cook and stir for about 7 minutes. Add broth and seasonings and simmer, covered, for 20 minutes. Stir in the apple.

Celery-Mushroom Stuffing

3 cups chopped celery
⅓ cup chicken broth
1 teaspoon salt
¼ teaspoon pepper
½ teaspoon thyme
½ teaspoon oregano *or* rosemary
3 cups chopped mushrooms (about ¾ pound)
2 tablespoons flour

Cook the celery in broth with the seasonings until almost tender. Add the mushrooms and cook a few minutes. Remove from heat and stir in the flour.

Potato Stuffing

       1 large onion, minced
       ¼ cup butter *or* margarine
       3 cups riced, cooked potatoes
       1 teaspoon salt
       ¼ teaspoon pepper
       ½ teaspoon thyme
       2 tablespoons minced parsley
       1 egg
       2 to 4 tablespoons milk

Cook the onion in the butter for 3 minutes. Add the next 5 in-gredients. Mix well. Add the egg, beaten with the 2 tablespoons of milk. Stir and add a little more milk if you want the stuffing more moist.

2 *Frying*

Fried chicken doesn't have to be Southern, although it is the most popular method below the Mason and Dixon line, every cook having her own variation. Maryland, Kentucky and Louisiana each offer excellent recipes.

Frying chickens are usually disjointed or cut up, seasoned, and coated with batter, or moistened in milk or beaten eggs and then dipped in flour, cracker meal or dry bread crumbs. The pieces are fried in a skillet in a fairly large quantity (usually from half an inch to two inches) of very hot vegetable shortening, lard or oil, until they are golden-crisp. Southern fried chicken is frequently served with cream gravy.

Fried Chicken

    2 broiler-fryers, about 3 pounds *each*, cut up
    ½ cup flour
    1½ teaspoons salt
    ¼ teaspoon pepper
    ⅛ teaspoon paprika
      Butter and shortening
    ½ cup water (optional)

Dredge the chicken with flour mixed with the salt, pepper, and paprika. Heat half butter and half oil in a heavy skillet to a depth of about ½". Brown the chicken for 20 minutes, turning to brown evenly. Add water, cover and steam for 15 minutes. Uncover and cook 5 minutes more to crisp skin and let the water boil off. (If you want a very crisp chicken, do not add water when you cover.) Makes 6 servings.

Spicy Fried Chicken

    1 broiler-fryer, 2½ to 3 pounds, quartered
    ¾ cup flour
    1 teaspoon salt
    ½ teaspoon pepper
    ¼ teaspoon *each* ginger and garlic powder
      Shortening
      Gravy (optional)

Rinse chicken and pat dry with paper toweling. Mix flour with seasonings and roll each piece in mixture. In chicken fryer or deep heavy skillet, heat shortening (to depth of 1" or more) until smoking hot. Using a pair of tongs, drop chicken in, cover and cook until golden brown on one side. Turn, cover and cook until golden brown on other side. Remove cover and cook until chicken is well browned on both sides. Reduce heat and fry slowly, turning once or twice, until fork-tender. When done, drain on paper toweling. Makes 4 servings.

Southern Fried Chicken

    2 broiler-fryers, about 3 pounds *each*, cut up
    ½ cup flour
    ½ teaspoon salt
    ¼ teaspoon pepper
    ⅛ teaspoon cayenne pepper
    6 tablespoons shortening
    2 cups milk
      Spoon cornbread *or* biscuits

Moisten the chicken slightly. Put the flour, salt, pepper and cayenne in a paper bag and shake the chicken in the bag, 2 or 3 pieces at a time. (Be sure each piece is thoroughly coated and reserve remaining seasoned flour.) Fry chicken in the shortening in a large skillet, turning to brown evenly, until cooked through and brown—about 25 minutes. Remove chicken and keep warm. Pour off the drippings, leaving about ¼ cup in the skillet. Add ¼ cup of the reserved seasoned flour, brown and blend. Pour in the milk slowly while stirring. Adjust seasoning and boil until thickened. This is especially good with spoon cornbread; biscuits will do. Makes 6 servings.

Southern Fried Chicken with Cream Gravy

        2 fryers, 2½ to 3 pounds *each*, cut up
    ¾ cup flour
        2 teaspoons salt
        1 teaspoon pepper
    ¼ cup butter
    ¼ cup shortening
        2 cups half-and-half

Shake the chicken in a bag with ½ cup of the flour combined with half the salt and pepper. Brown the chicken over high heat in a mixture of butter and shortening. Turn to brown on all sides. Cover and continue to cook slowly for ½ hour, removing the cover for the last 10 minutes. Remove the chicken, pour off all but about 3 tablespoons of fat and blend in the remaining flour, salt, and pepper. Add the half-and-half slowly while stirring. Stir and cook until smooth and thickened and pour over the chicken. Makes 6 servings.

Southern Bacon-Fried Chicken

2 broiler-fryers, about 2½ pounds *each*, cut up
¼ cup flour
½ teaspoon salt
¼ teaspoon pepper
Bacon fat
1 cup milk
1 tablespoon minced parsley

Shake the chicken pieces in a paper bag with a mixture of the flour, salt and pepper, reserving excess. Heat bacon fat about 1" deep in a large skillet. When hot, fry the chicken a few pieces at a time. Turn to brown evenly and set aside as you fry remaining pieces. Return all the pieces to the pan, reduce heat, and cook about half an hour, turning the chicken frequently. Remove to a hot platter and keep warm. Pour off all but about 2 tablespoons fat, blend in the remaining seasoned flour, brown, and pour in the milk slowly while stirring. Bring to a boil and simmer 2 or 3 minutes. If gravy is too thick, add a little more milk. Sprinkle in the parsley. Spoon a little over the chicken if you wish and pass the rest. Makes 6 servings.

Fried Buttermilk Chicken

1½ cups flour
2 teaspoons salt
2 teaspoons paprika
½ teaspoon pepper
2 broiler-fryers, about 3 pounds *each*, cut up
1 cup buttermilk
Fat for deep frying

Combine the flour, salt, paprika and pepper. Dip the chicken pieces in buttermilk and then roll in the flour mixture. Fry in deep hot fat (375°) for about 10 minutes. If you don't fry it all at once drain on paper toweling as you go and keep warm. Put all the pieces in a baking pan, cover and bake at 350° for 30 minutes. Makes 6 servings.

Easy Fried Chicken

    1 broiler-fryer, 3 to 3½ pounds, cut up
    ¾ cup flour
    1 teaspoon salt
    ¼ teaspoon pepper
    1 teaspoon baking powder
    Oil *or* fat for deep frying

Wash the chicken but do not dry. Combine flour, salt, pepper and baking powder. Dip the wet chicken in the flour mixture, coating thoroughly on all sides. Fry in deep fat. Drain on paper toweling. Makes 4 servings.

Cornmeal Batter-Fried Chicken

    ¾ cup cornmeal
    ½ cup flour
    1 teaspoon salt
    ¼ teaspoon pepper
    1 teaspoon thyme, sage *or* poultry seasoning
    1 cup milk
    1 egg
    2 broiler-fryers, 2½ to 3 pounds *each*, cut up
    Fat for frying

Mix the dry ingredients together, add the milk and egg, and beat until thoroughly blended. Dip the chicken in the batter, coating it on all sides. Fry in hot fat (375°) for 10 minutes, turning to brown evenly. Drain on paper toweling. Makes 6 servings.

Corn-Crisp Chicken

    1½ cups cornflake crumbs
      2 teaspoons monosodium glutamate
      2 teaspoons salt
     ¼ teaspoon pepper
      2 broiler-fryers, 2½ to 3 pounds *each*, cut up
     ¾ cup evaporated milk

Mix first 4 ingredients. Line large shallow baking pan with foil.
Dip chicken pieces in the milk, then roll in crumb mixture.
Put, skin side up, in pan. Bake at 350° 1 hour. This low-calorie
chicken tastes like fried. Makes 6 servings.

Crumb-Fried Chicken

      2 broiler-fryers, about 2½ pounds *each*, cut up
    1½ cups milk
      1 cup flour
      2 teaspoons salt
      2 eggs
      3 cups bread crumbs
        Fat for frying

Moisten the chicken with 1 cup of the milk and coat with the
flour mixed with the salt. Beat the eggs with the remaining ½
cup milk and dip chicken pieces in it. Turn in the bread crumbs,
being sure all sides are coated. Meanwhile heat fat about
1″ deep to 360° and fry the chicken, turning with tongs to
brown evenly. Cover and cook over low heat for 15 minutes.
Then cook uncovered for 15 minutes more to ensure the
chicken's being crisp. Makes 6 servings.

Maryland Fried Chicken

> 2 broiler-fryers, 2½ to 3 pounds *each*, cut up
> 1 cup flour
> 2 teaspoons salt
> ½ teaspoon pepper
> ½ cup butter *or* margarine
> 2 cups milk
> ½ cup heavy cream

Shake the chicken in a bag with the flour, salt and pepper, reserving excess. Brown in butter, turning to brown on all sides. When brown, cover and cook over low heat for 35 minutes. Drain and keep warm. Blend remaining 5 or 6 tablespoons seasoned flour into the drippings. Stir in the milk and cream and simmer and stir until thickened and smooth. Taste for seasoning. Pass the gravy or pour some over the chicken and pass the rest. Makes 6 servings.

Louisiana Fried Chicken

> 2 broiler-fryers, about 2½ pounds *each*, cut up
> 2 cups milk
> 1 cup flour
> 2 teaspoons salt
> ½ teaspoon pepper
> 3 eggs, beaten
> 1 cup cracker meal
> Fat for frying

Soak the chicken in milk for 30 to 60 minutes. Shake in a bag in a mixture of the flour, salt and pepper. Combine the eggs with ¾ cup of the milk, dip the chicken in the mixture and then roll in cracker meal mixed with a little of the seasoned flour. Fry in deep fat at 350° for about 20 minutes, until brown. Turn pieces while frying and do not fry too many at a time.

Remove as they're done, drain on paper toweling, and keep warm. Serve with Cream Gravy (see below) if you wish. Makes 6 servings.

Kentucky Fried Chicken

>   2 broiler-fryers, 2½ to 3 pounds *each*, cut up
>   1 teaspoon salt
>   1½ teaspoons baking powder
>   1 cup flour
>   Fat for deep frying
>   Cream Gravy (optional; see below)

Rinse the chicken but do not dry. Combine the salt and baking powder with the flour. Dip the wet pieces of chicken in this, coating heavily on all sides. Fry in deep fat for about 25 minutes, until golden and tender. In parts of the South, fried chicken is served with Cream Gravy. Makes 6 servings.

Cream Gravy

>   ¼ cup flour
>   ¼ cup drippings and fat chicken was fried in
>   2 cups half-and-half *or* part heavy cream
>   Salt and pepper

Add ¼ cup flour to drippings and fat and stir well. Pour in half-and-half slowly while stirring steadily. Season to taste with salt and pepper. For a richer gravy, use part heavy cream.

Skillet Chicken

> 1 frying chicken, 2½ to 3 pounds, cut up
> 2 teaspoons salt
> ¼ teaspoon pepper
> ¼ cup olive oil
> ⅓ cup green onion, including tops, chopped
> 1 small clove garlic, minced
> ¼ cup finely chopped parsley
> ½ teaspoon marjoram, crushed
> ½ cup lemon juice
> Water

Sprinkle chicken with the salt and pepper. Heat oil in large skillet, add chicken and brown thoroughly over moderate heat—this takes about 10 minutes altogether. Sprinkle chicken with all the other ingredients except water, turning so seasoning is on all sides. Cover and simmer over very low heat until chicken is tender, about 30 minutes. Turn chicken pieces occasionally with tongs, and as the pan juices evaporate, add water, about ¼ cup, stirring up the bits stuck to the bottom of the pan. Makes 4 servings.

Skillet Fried Chicken

> 1 broiler-fryer, 2½ to 3 pounds, cut up
> Salt and pepper to taste
> Flour
> Oil, shortening *or* lard for frying

Sprinkle chicken with salt and pepper; coat with flour. In large skillet heat ½ inch oil (about 2½ cups) over medium-high heat to about 375°. Add chicken, skin side down, placing larger pieces in center. Fry 10 minutes or until crisp and golden; cover and cook 5 minutes longer. Turn chicken, reduce heat to medium, cover and cook 10 minutes. Uncover and cook 5 minutes to crisp skin. Remove chicken and drain on paper toweling. Makes 4 servings.

Picnic Fried Chicken

⅔ cup evaporated milk
1 cup flour
1½ teaspoons salt
1 teaspoon paprika
⅛ teaspoon pepper
1 teaspoon poultry seasoning
Vegetable oil for frying
2 broiler-fryers, 2½ to 3 pounds *each*, cut in serving
pieces

Put milk in shallow bowl. Mix flour and seasonings in another
shallow bowl. Heat ½" oil in each of 2 large skillets. Dip chicken
pieces in the milk, then roll in flour mixture. Using tongs to avoid
piercing meat, drop chicken gently into hot oil. Fry over medium
heat 15 to 20 minutes on each side. Chill. Makes 6 servings.

Almost Fried Chicken

1 broiler-fryer, about 3 pounds, cut up
½ cup flour
1 teaspoon salt
⅛ teaspoon pepper
1 teaspoon paprika
⅓ cup margarine

Shake chicken pieces in mixture of flour and seasonings in plastic
or paper bag until well coated. Put margarine in shallow baking
pan and melt in preheated 400° oven. Put chicken in pan and
turn to coat with margarine. Bake, skin side down, 30 minutes.
Turn and bake about 30 minutes longer. Makes 4 servings.

3 *Sautéeing*

Sautéed chicken, whole or cut up, is also cooked in a skillet but at a lower temperature than fried, and in a much smaller quantity of shortening, butter or margarine being the most appropriate fats. The pieces may be lightly coated with seasoned flour, either by dredging or by shaking in a paper bag. Like frying, sautéeing is a quick and easy way of preparing chicken, with herbs and seasoning lending variety to suit individual tastes.

Basic Sautéed Chicken

> 2 broiler-fryers, 2½ to 3 pounds *each*, quartered
> 1 teaspoon salt
> ¼ teaspoon pepper
> ¼ cup butter
> ¼ cup water

Wash the chicken and dry thoroughly. Sprinkle with salt and pepper and sauté in butter in a heavy skillet for about 15 minutes, turning to brown evenly. Add the water, cover and cook 15 minutes. Most of the water will be gone. Remove cover, turn the pieces, add a little more butter if necessary, and sauté 5 to 10 minutes more. Makes 6 servings.

Herbed Chicken Sautéed with Wine

> 2 broiler-fryers, about 3 pounds *each*, quartered
> 1 teaspoon salt
> ¼ teaspoon pepper
> ¼ cup butter
> 1 onion, minced
> 1 tablespoon minced chives
> 1 tablespoon minced parsley
> 1 teaspoon tarragon *and/or* rosemary
> ½ cup white wine

Wash and dry the chicken. Sprinkle with salt and pepper and sauté in butter. Add the onion and cook gently for 10 minutes. Add the herbs, stir, add the wine and simmer, covered, for 20 minutes. Makes 6 servings.

Sautéed Chicken Chasseur

> 2 broiler-fryers, 3 to 3½ pounds *each*, quartered
> 2 tablespoons flour
> 2 teaspoons salt
> ¼ teaspoon pepper
> 3 tablespoons butter
> 6 scallions, chopped
> 1 tablespoon lemon juice
> ¼ cup white wine
> 2 or 3 tomatoes, peeled and diced
> 1 teaspoon sugar
> 1 tablespoon minced parsley

Sprinkle the chicken with a mixture of flour, 1 teaspoon salt, and the pepper. Add butter to pan and lightly brown over medium heat. Sauté chicken in browned butter for 10 minutes, turning to brown evenly. Add the scallions, cover and simmer 5 minutes. Combine the lemon juice and wine and pour over. Cover and simmer 5 minutes. Add tomatoes, sugar, and remaining salt and simmer for about 20 minutes until chicken is tender. Serve sprinkled with parsley. Makes 6 to 8 servings.

Lemon Chicken Sauté

      2 broiler-fryers, about 3 pounds *each*, quartered
      6 tablespoons butter
      1 teaspoon salt
   ¼ teaspoon pepper
      2 tablespoons lemon juice
        Grated rind of 1 lemon
      2 tablespoons water
      2 tablespoons chopped parsley

Wash and dry the chicken and sauté in 4 tablespoons butter, turning to brown evenly. Add salt and pepper. Cover and cook gently for 15 minutes. Brown remaining butter, add lemon juice and rind and pour over the chicken. Cover and cook 10 to 15 minutes, until tender. Remove chicken to a warm platter. Add water to the skillet, scrape up brown bits, bring to a boil and pour over the chicken. Sprinkle with parsley. Makes 6 to 8 servings.

Chicken Sauté with Red Wine and Nuts

> 2 broiler-fryers, 2½ to 3 pounds *each*, cut up
> 1 teaspoon salt
> ½ teaspoon pepper
> ¼ cup butter
> 1 medium onion, chopped fine
> 1 teaspoon chervil *or* tarragon
> ½ cup chicken broth
> 1 cup red wine
> 1 to 2 tablespoons flour
> ½ cup slivered almonds *or* chopped pecans

Sprinkle the chickens with salt and pepper and sauté in butter, turning to brown evenly. After 10 minutes, add onion, herb, broth and wine. Cover and simmer half an hour or until the chicken is tender. Remove chicken to a warm platter and keep warm. Add flour and bring sauce to a boil. When smooth and slightly thickened, add the nuts. Pour over the chicken. Makes 6 servings.

Sautéed Chicken with Apple

> 1 broiler-fryer, 3 to 3½ pounds, quartered
> 1 teaspoon salt
> 3 tablespoons butter *or* margarine
> 1 apple, peeled, cored and diced
> 1 tablespoon apple jelly
> ¼ cup white wine *or* apple cider

Dry the chicken and sprinkle with salt. Sauté in butter, turning to brown evenly. After about 15 minutes add the apple, jelly and wine. Cover and simmer for 20 minutes. Uncover and simmer about 10 minutes, until the chicken is tender. Makes 4 servings.

Sautéed Chicken with Almonds

        2 cups diced raw chicken
        3 tablespoons oil
        1 teaspoon salt
        2 tablespoons soy sauce
        1 cup diced celery
        1 small onion, minced
        ¼ pound mushrooms, sliced
        ⅓ cup water
        1 tablespoon cornstarch *or* arrowroot
        ½ cup toasted almonds

Sauté the chicken in oil for 4 or 5 minutes. Add salt and soy
and stir. Add the celery, onion, mushrooms and water. Cover and
simmer 5 minutes. Blend the cornstarch with a little water and
stir in. Cook and stir until thickened and clear. Sprinkle with
almonds. Makes 4 servings.

Quick Skillet Chicken

        3 chicken breasts, totaling about 2½ pounds, split
     1½ teaspoons salt
        ¾ teaspoon monosodium glutamate
        ¾ teaspoon thyme
        3 tablespoons butter *or* margarine
        1 package (10 ounces) frozen peas
        ½ cup diagonally sliced celery
        1 small onion, chopped
        ⅔ cup water
        1 chicken bouillon cube
        1 can (13¼ ounces) pineapple chunks, undrained
     1½ tablespoons cornstarch blended with 2 tablespoons
             water and 2 teaspoons Worcestershire sauce
        1 tomato, peeled and cut in 6 to 8 wedges
          Hot cooked brown or white rice

Skin and bone chicken and cut meat in strips (about 10 to each breast half). Sprinkle with salt, monosodium glutamate and thyme. Sauté strips in hot butter for 3 minutes. Add peas and break up with fork. Add celery and onion and cook and stir 2 minutes. Add water, bouillon cube and pineapple. Bring to boil, reduce heat, cover and cook 4 minutes. Stir in cornstarch mixture and cook and stir until thickened. Add tomato wedges and serve over rice. Makes 6 servings.

Skillet Chicken and Rice

      ¼ cup flour
    1½ teaspoons salt
     1 teaspoon paprika
     ¼ teaspoon pepper
     1 broiler-fryer, about 3 pounds, cut up
     ¼ cup margarine *or* other fat
     1 medium onion, sliced
     ¾ cup raw white or brown rice

Mix flour, 1 teaspoon salt, the paprika and pepper. Dredge chicken pieces with the mixture and sauté in the margarine in skillet until browned on both sides. Pour off most of fat. Add 2 cups water, remaining salt, onion and rice. Stir with fork, bring to boil and simmer, covered, 30 minutes, or until rice and chicken are tender and liquid is absorbed. Makes 4 servings.

4 *Broiling*

Few dishes are better and easier to prepare than broiled chicken. Broilers, which weigh from 1½ to 2½ pounds, should be split, cut in half, or quartered, according to size (the birds' and the appetites'). They require nothing but seasoning; however, you may brush them with melted butter or oil. Then place them, skin side down, in the rack of the broiler pan, about 5″ from the preheated unit. After 15 to 20 minutes, turn them skin side up, brush with more shortening, if desired, and broil for another 15 minutes or until brown. Placing the pan closer to or farther from the heat will speed up or slow down the browning process.

Tarragon-Lemon Broiled Chicken

>   6 tablespoons butter
>   3 tablespoons lemon juice
>   2 broiler-fryers, 3 to 3½ pounds *each,* quartered
>   1 teaspoon salt
>   ¼ teaspoon pepper
>   2 tablespoons fresh chopped tarragon *or*
>   3 teaspoons dried
>   Lemon wedges

Melt half the butter in a shallow pan. Add half the lemon juice. Put the chicken in the butter, skin side down. Brush top of chicken with remaining butter, melted, and remaining lemon juice. Combine salt, pepper and tarragon and sprinkle half on the chicken. Broil for 20 minutes. Turn, sprinkle with remaining herbs and broil 20 minutes more, until chicken is tender and brown. Serve with lemon wedges. Makes 6 to 8 servings.

Fat-Free Broiled Chicken

>   2 broiler-fryers, about 2 pounds *each,* split
>   1½ teaspoons salt
>   ¼ teaspoon pepper

Put the chickens, skin side down, about 4″ from the heat. Broil for 20 minutes, sprinkle with a little salt and pepper, turn and broil, skin side up, for 15 minutes. Sprinkle with remaining salt and pepper and serve at once. Certainly you may rub or brush with butter or oil if you wish, but it is not necessary. Makes 4 servings.

Apple Broiled Chicken

    2 broilers, 2 to 2½ pounds *each*, split
  ¼ cup butter, melted
    1 teaspoon salt
    1 cup apple cider
     Apple jelly *or* applesauce

Brush the chickens with butter and sprinkle with salt. Place in broiler, skin side down, and fill the cavities with cider. Broil 20 minutes, brushing with cider. Turn, broil 20 minutes more, brushing several times with the cider. Serve with any remaining cider heated and poured over. Pass apple jelly or applesauce. Makes 4 servings.

Broiled Mustard-and-Honey-Glazed Chicken

     Garlic salt to taste
    1 broiler-fryer, 3 pounds, quartered
    2 tablespoons prepared mustard
  ⅓ cup honey blended with juice of 1 lime (about 3
      tablespoons)

Sprinkle garlic salt generously on both sides of chicken. Place, skin side down, on broiler pan, spread with 1 tablespoon mustard and broil 20 minutes, basting twice with half the honey mixture during last 10 minutes. Turn chicken skin side up, spread with remaining 1 tablespoon mustard and broil 20 minutes or until chicken is tender, basting twice with remaining honey mixture during last 10 minutes. Makes 4 servings.

Broiled Chicken Thighs with Blue Cheese

       1 package blue-cheese salad-dressing mix
       ⅔ cup salad oil
         Juice and grated rind of 1 lemon
       2 tablespoons water
       8 chicken thighs

Mix well first 4 ingredients. Place thighs in shallow dish or pie-pan and pour mixture over all. Marinate about 1 hour, then broil 6″ from heat 10 minutes on each side, or until well browned. Baste frequently with marinade until all is used. Makes 4 servings.

5 *Fricasseeing*

Good old-fashioned chicken fricassee is simply a fowl, usually cut in pieces, simmered in water until fork-tender. It may be served with potatoes, rice or noodles, dumplings or spaetzle, or on hot biscuits, toast or cornbread. The gravy—golden, savory and with a definite chicken flavor—should be slightly thickened with flour, cornstarch or arrowroot. This dish is popular with thrifty housewives, being made from elderly birds that are cheaper than their younger cousins. In addition, after the gravy has been made there will be "dividends" in the form of broth and fat for use in future recipes. (Fricassee may be made from young chickens and chicken parts as well as the older "hens." The cooking time is then shorter.)

Chicken Fricassee

> 1 stewing chicken, 4 to 5 pounds, cut up
> 3 cups hot water
> 2 sprigs parsley
> Salt
> ¼ teaspoon white pepper
> 2 stalks celery
> 1 medium onion
> 1 bay leaf
> 3 tablespoons flour
> ¼ cup milk
> Lemon juice
> Paprika

Put chicken pieces in large heavy kettle. Add the water, parsley, 1½ teaspoons salt and next 4 ingredients. Bring to boil, cover and simmer about 2 hours. Remove chicken, strain broth and skim off fat. Return 2 cups broth to kettle. Blend flour and milk, stir gradually into broth and simmer a few minutes. Add chicken and heat gently. Season with salt and lemon juice to taste. Arrange chicken and gravy on platter. Sprinkle with paprika. Makes 4 to 6 servings.

Golden Fricassee with Potatoes

> 1 hen, 5 pounds, cut up
> Water
> 5 to 7 tablespoons prepared yellow or brown
>   mustard
> 2 teaspoons salt
> 12 to 14 new potatoes
> ½ pint sour cream or heavy cream

Put the chicken in a large pot and cover with water. Add about 5 tablespoons of mustard and the salt. Cover and simmer until

tender. The time will vary depending upon the age of the bird—
2 to 2½ hours. About 35 minutes before serving, add the potatoes.
When they are done, reduce heat and stir in the cream. Do not
boil. Taste for seasoning—you may need more salt and mustard.
You may thicken with a little flour-and-water paste before adding
the cream if you want a really thick sauce. Makes 6 servings.

Quick Chicken Fricassee

> 1 roasting chicken, 3½ to 4 pounds, cut up
> 2 cups water
> 1 onion
> 1 stalk celery
> 1 carrot
> 1 teaspoon salt
>   Parsley
> 1 envelope (⅞ ounce) chicken-gravy mix

Put chicken pieces in heavy kettle with water, next 4 ingredients
and 2 sprigs parsley. Bring to boil, cover and simmer 1 hour,
or until tender. Remove chicken, strain broth and skim off fat.
Return 2 cups broth to kettle. Add gravy mix, stir, bring to boil
and simmer a few minutes. Return chicken to gravy and heat.
Sprinkle with chopped parsley. Makes 4 servings.

Chicken Fricassee with Vegetables

> 4 chicken hindquarters
> ⅓ cup flour
>   Salt and pepper
> 2 tablespoons margarine
> 1 medium onion, quartered and sliced
> 1 can chicken gravy *or* chicken-giblet gravy
> ¾ cup water
> 4 potatoes, diced
> 1 can (1 pound) cut green beans, drained

Dust chicken with flour mixed with ½ teaspoon salt and ¼ teaspoon pepper and brown in the margarine in heavy kettle. Add onion and cook until lightly browned. Stir in gravy and water and simmer 40 minutes, or until chicken is tender. Add potatoes and simmer 15 minutes, or just until done. Add beans and simmer until heated through. Taste and correct seasoning, if necessary. Makes 4 servings.

Fricassee of Wings

        12 to 14 chicken wings
        1 onion stuck with 2 cloves
        1 bay leaf
        1 teaspoon salt
          A few celery leaves
        1 or 2 parsley sprigs
          Water
        3 tablespoons butter
        4 tablespoons flour
        ½ cup heavy cream
          Salt, pepper and nutmeg
          Lemon juice
          Chopped parsley
          Hot cooked rice

Put first 6 ingredients in pan with water barely to cover (about 3 cups). Bring to boil, skim off scum, then reduce heat and simmer about 1 hour, or until just tender. Remove wings and keep warm. Strain and measure broth. Melt butter in saucepan and blend in flour. Gradually stir in 1½ cups strained broth and cook, stirring, until thickened. Mix in cream and season to taste with salt, pepper and nutmeg. Add a good squeeze of lemon juice and a little chopped parsley. Put wings into sauce and reheat. Serve over rice. Makes 4 servings.

Liver Fricassee

> 1 medium onion, sliced
> ¼ cup butter *or* margarine
> 1 pound chicken livers
> 1 can condensed cream of mushroom soup
> ⅔ cup milk
> ¼ teaspoon thyme
>   Chopped parsley

Sauté onion in the butter 2 to 3 minutes. Add livers and cook, stirring, about 4 minutes. Add soup, milk and thyme. Heat gently, stirring. Sprinkle with parsley. Makes 4 servings.

Chicken Stew

> 4 whole chicken breasts, split
> 2 tablespoons butter
> 2 tablespoons oil
> 2 teaspoons salt
> ¼ teaspoon thyme
> ¼ teaspoon tarragon
> 3 tablespoons flour
> 2 cups water
> 16 white boiling onions
> ¾ to 1 pound mushrooms, cut up if large

Brown the chicken in a mixture of the butter and oil. Turn to brown evenly. Remove the chicken. Combine the salt and herbs with flour. Add to the skillet and blend. Pour in water slowly; bring to a boil while stirring. Add the onions and chicken. Cover and simmer for half an hour. Add mushrooms and cook 10 minutes. Makes 8 servings.

Southern Chicken Stew

    2 broiler-fryers, about 3 pounds *each*, cut up
    2 tablespoons butter
    2 tablespoons oil
    1 cup chopped onion
    3 tablespoons tomato paste
    ½ cup hot water
    1 teaspoon salt
    ½ teaspoon pepper
    ½ teaspoon oregano
    2 packages (10 ounces *each*) frozen whole okra

Sauté the chicken in a mixture of butter and oil until light brown. Simmer covered for 20 minutes; remove and keep warm. Sauté the onion in the drippings. Mix the tomato paste with the hot water and stir in. Return chicken to the pot and season with salt, pepper, and oregano; stir well and add okra. Simmer covered for 25 minutes. Makes 6 servings.

Kentucky Mulligan Stew

    1 roasting chicken or hen, about 4 pounds
      Salt
    1 pound beef, cut into cubes
    2 tablespoons bacon drippings *or* fat
    3 onions, sliced
    ¼ cup flour
    1 (1 pound) can tomatoes
    1 (1 pound) can whole kernel corn
    1 package (10 ounces) frozen peas
    1 package (10 ounces) frozen baby lima beans
    ¼ teaspoon pepper
    ¼ teaspoon paprika
    3 tablespoons sherry

If you use a hen, simmer it in salted water to cover for about 2½ hours, until tender. Remove meat from bones and reserve the liquid. If you use a roasting chicken, simmer it in salted water for 45 minutes. Brown the beef in the bacon drippings or fat, add the onions and brown. Sprinkle with a teaspoon of salt and the flour, add 3 cups of the broth the chicken was cooked in and stir. Add the tomatoes, corn, peas, lima beans, pepper, paprika, and the chicken and simmer covered for about 15 minutes. Adjust seasoning to taste, thicken with a little flour-and-water paste if you wish, add the sherry and simmer a few minutes more. Makes 6 to 8 servings.

Brunswick Stew

      1 chicken, about 4½ pounds, cut up
      4 cups water
   1½ teaspoons salt
      ¼ teaspoon pepper
      1 medium onion, minced
      1 can (1 pound) tomatoes
      2 tablespoons sherry
      1 tablespoon Worcestershire sauce
      1 cup frozen *or* canned okra
      1 package (10 ounces) frozen lima beans
      1 package (10 ounces) frozen whole kernel corn
         Flour (optional)

Put the chicken in a large heavy pot with next 7 ingredients. Cover and simmer for about 45 minutes, until the chicken is almost tender. Add the okra and lima beans and cook for 15 minutes. Add corn and cook for 10 minutes. Thicken juices with a little flour-and-water paste if you wish. If you prefer, before adding the vegetables you may cool the chicken, remove skin and bones and cut it into bite-size pieces. Return it to the pot and add the vegetables as above. Makes 6 servings.

Fricassee with Dumplings

>   1 hen, about 5 pounds, cut up
>   4 cups water
>   1 carrot, cut up
>   1 onion, cut up
>   2 stalks celery, cut up
>   2 bay leaves
>   2 teaspoons salt
>   ½ teaspoon pepper
>   Dumplings, made with biscuit mix

Put all of the ingredients except the dumplings in a large kettle, bring to a boil, and simmer 2½ to 3 hours, until the chicken is tender. Make dumplings according to package directions and drop by spoonfuls on top of the chicken. Cover and cook 12 minutes. Uncover and cook 5 minutes. Makes 6 servings.

Chicken and Dumplings

>   1 broiler-fryer, about 3 pounds, cut up
>   Water
>   2 teaspoons salt
>   ¼ teaspoon pepper
>   2 celery stalks
>   1 onion, sliced
>   2 carrots, coarsely chopped
>   1 sprig parsley
>   1 bay leaf
>   2 chicken bouillon cubes
>   ½ cup milk
>   ⅓ cup flour
>   2 egg yolks, beaten
>   Parsley Dumplings (see following)

Put chicken in kettle or Dutch oven and cover with boiling water. Add next 8 ingredients, bring to boil, cover and simmer 1¼ hours, or until chicken is tender. Remove chicken from liquid and, when cool enough to handle, remove meat from bones. Measure liquid and if more than 4 cups, boil down to 4 cups. Blend milk and flour. Gradually add a little hot liquid to milk, then stir milk into remaining hot liquid and cook, stirring, until thickened. With spoon, gradually beat in egg yolks. Put chicken back in broth. Drop dumpling batter by tablespoonfuls into bubbling broth. Cook, uncovered, 10 minutes. Cover and cook 10 minutes longer. Makes 4 servings.

Parsley Dumplings

> 1 cup all-purpose flour
> 2 teaspoons baking powder
> ½ teaspoon *each* sugar, salt and celery seed
> 1 tablespoon chopped parsley
> ½ cup milk

Mix together flour, baking powder, sugar, salt, celery seed and chopped parsley. With fork, stir in milk until just moistened.

Poached Chicken with Tarragon

> 1 hen or roaster, about 5 pounds, cut up
> 3 cups broth
> 1 tablespoon fresh tarragon *or* 2 teaspoons dried
> 3 scallions, minced
> 2 tablespoons minced parsley
> 3 tablespoons flour
> 3 tablespoons water
> 3 tablespoons heavy cream
>   Cooked rice or noodles

Put the chicken in a pot with broth and half the tarragon. Cover and simmer until tender—1½ to 3 hours, depending upon the age of the bird. Remove chicken. Add scallions and parsley to the broth, cover and simmer 10 minutes. Combine flour and water, stir in and cook 2 minutes. Return chicken to the pot and reheat for about 10 minutes. Put the chicken on a warm platter. Add cream and remaining tarragon to the gravy and adjust seasoning. Pour a little over the chicken and pass the rest. Serve with rice or noodles. Makes 6 servings.

Poached Chicken with Carrots, Rice and Lemon Sauce

    1 roasting chicken, 4 to 5 pounds
    2 quarts water
    1 tablespoon salt
    1 medium onion
    1 bay leaf
    2 parsley sprigs
    4 large carrots, cut in chunks
      Lemon Sauce (see below)
      Cooked rice

Put chicken in Dutch oven; add water, salt, onion, bay leaf and parsley and bring to boil. Cover and simmer 30 minutes. Add carrots and continue to simmer until chicken and carrots are tender (about 20 minutes). Remove chicken and carrots to heated platter and keep warm. Strain broth. Prepare Lemon Sauce and serve over carved chicken, carrots and rice. Makes 4 to 6 servings.

Lemon Sauce

    3 tablespoons butter *or* margarine
    3 tablespoons flour
    2 cups chicken broth
    1 egg yolk mixed with ¼ cup half-and-half
    2 tablespoons lemon juice
      Salt to taste

In saucepan melt butter, blend in flour and gradually add broth. Cook and stir until thickened and smooth. Stir in egg mixture and cook and stir 1 minute. Add lemon juice and salt.

Chicken with Walnuts

> 1 chicken, 3 to 4 pounds, cut up
> ¼ cup butter
> 1 teaspoon salt
> ¼ teaspoon pepper
> 6 to 8 scallions, chopped
> 2 tablespoons lemon juice
> ¼ cup water
> ¼ cup dry sherry
> 1 cup cream
> ¼ pound walnuts, chopped

Brown the chicken in butter, turning to brown evenly. Sprinkle with salt and pepper. Add the scallions and cook 2 minutes. Add lemon juice, water and sherry. Simmer covered for about half an hour, or until the chicken is tender. Add the cream and walnuts; heat through but do not boil. Makes 4 to 6 servings.

Boiled Chicken with Rice

>   1 stewing chicken, about 5 pounds
>   Water
>   1 carrot, cut in chunks
>   2 celery stalks and tops, cut in pieces
>   2 parsley sprigs
>   1 large onion, sliced
>   1 clove garlic
>   1 teaspoon salt
>   1 cup raw rice
>   ¼ cup butter
>   ⅓ cup flour
>   1 cup half-and-half

Put chicken in kettle with enough water to come halfway over chicken. Add next 6 ingredients. Cover and simmer for 2½ hours, or until chicken is tender. About 30 minutes before chicken is cooked, remove 2 cups chicken broth and strain. Cook rice in this until tender, about 20 minutes. Rice should be moist. When chicken is tender, remove to a warm platter and keep warm. Strain 2 cups broth. Melt butter and blend in flour. Add 2 cups broth and cook, stirring, until smooth and thickened. Stir in half-and-half. Simmer for about 10 minutes. Serve chicken on bed of rice. Spoon some of the sauce over the chicken and pass the remainder on the side. Makes 6 to 8 servings.

6 *Casseroles*

Casseroles are a great help to the hostess. They not only can, but should, be made ahead of time, actually tasting better if they are cooked a day in advance and reheated. Their usually being one-dish meals makes them particularly convenient for family or party fare—for practically any type of entertaining, from brunch to after-the-theater, especially at buffets where fork-food is indicated.

Special equipment is not necessary; any low, ovenproof pot with a tight-fitting lid will do, whether it is earthenware, glass, cast iron, enamel, copper or stainless steel. A casserole comes to the table in the dish it was cooked in, so a handsome container is an asset; but it is not essential, for once the lid has been removed, the contents of a chicken casserole will delight the eye as well as the nose of the most fastidious guest.

Chicken Casserole

> 1 broiler-fryer, 3 to 3½ pounds, cut up or left whole
> 2 teaspoons salt
> 2 tablespoons minced onion
> 2 tablespoons butter *or* margarine
> ¼ cup flour
> ¼ teaspoon pepper
> 1 teaspoon paprika
> 2 cups half-and-half
> ¼ cup sherry
> 1 package (10 ounces) frozen peas
> ½ pound mushrooms, cut up
> 1 cup sour cream

Simmer the chicken in water almost to cover with 1 teaspoon of the salt for about 40 minutes, until tender. Remove meat from bones in large pieces and place in a baking dish. Sauté the onion in butter until light brown; stir in the flour, remaining salt, pepper and paprika. Stir and cook 1 minute. Add the half-and-half and cook while stirring about 3 minutes, until thickened and smooth. Add the sherry, peas and mushrooms, and cook 3 minutes. Add the sour cream, stir and pour over the chicken in the baking dish. Bake at 350° for about 15 minutes, until heated through and bubbly. Makes 6 servings.

Chicken-Rice Casserole

> 1 broiler-fryer, about 3½ pounds, cut up
> Salt
> 1 onion, cut up
> 1 stalk celery
> Few parsley sprigs
> 1 cup raw rice
> 2 cups chopped celery
> 4 eggs, beaten
> 1½ cups milk
> ½ teaspoon *each* dried onion and parsley flakes
> Pepper to taste

Put chicken in kettle with 2 cups water, 1 teaspoon salt and next 3 ingredients. Bring to boil, cover and simmer 45 minutes, or until almost tender. Remove chicken and cool. Strain broth. Remove chicken meat from bones. Mix chicken, broth and remaining ingredients. Add salt to taste. Put in a casserole and bake at 350° for 40 minutes. Makes 6 servings.

Exotic Chicken and Rice Casserole

> 2 frying chickens, 2 to 3 pounds *each*, cut up
> ½ cup butter *or* margarine
> 2 medium green peppers, chopped
> 1 clove garlic, minced
> 2 onions, chopped
> 1 can (1 pound) tomatoes
> ½ cup seedless raisins
> ½ cup slivered almonds
> 1 teaspoon curry powder
> 1 teaspoon thyme
> Salt and pepper to taste
> 2 cups rice, partially cooked

Sauté chicken in the butter until golden brown. Remove to a large casserole. Pour off butter and put next 4 ingredients, ¼ cup each raisins and almonds, the curry powder, thyme, salt and pepper to taste in skillet. Simmer 10 to 15 minutes. Put rice in casserole with chicken and pour the hot mixture over top. Cover and bake at 400° 30 minutes, or until chicken is tender. Sprinkle with remaining raisins and almonds. Makes 6 servings.

California Chicken with Rice and Olives

          1 chicken, 4 to 5 pounds, cut up
        ¼ cup oil (can be part chicken fat)
          2 cups raw rice
          1 tablespoon minced parsley
          1 tablespoon minced chives
          1 to 2 teaspoons salt
          3 bay leaves
          1 cup water
        1½ cups chicken broth
        ½ cup black seeded olives
        ½ cup green seeded olives

Sauté the chicken in oil, turning to brown on all sides. Remove chicken. Add rice, parsley, chives, salt and bay leaves to the drippings and stir and brown for a few minutes. Pour in the water and then the broth while stirring. Return chicken to the pot and simmer, covered, for about 45 minutes, until the chicken is tender. Add the olives and reheat. Makes 6 servings.

Chicken, Macaroni and Green Peas

    1 broiler-fryer, 2½ to 3 pounds, cut up
    2 tablespoons oil
    1 medium onion, coarsely chopped
    1 cup uncooked elbow macaroni
    1 can (10¾ ounces) cream of chicken *or* cream of
        mushroom soup diluted with 1½ soup-cans water
    1 package (10 ounces) frozen peas
    ½ teaspoon salt
      Pepper to taste

Brown chicken in oil; push to one side of skillet. Add onion and sauté until tender. Stir in macaroni and add diluted soup, making sure soup covers macaroni. Rearrange chicken on macaroni, top with peas and season with salt and pepper. Cover and cook over medium heat 20 minutes or until macaroni is tender and chicken done. Makes 4 servings.

Lemon Chicken

    1 chicken, about 4 pounds, cut up
    ¼ cup butter
      Water
    1½ teaspoons salt
    ½ cup white wine
      Juice and grated rind of 1 lemon
    2 tablespoons sherry
    1 cup heavy cream
    1 lemon, sliced very thin
    ¼ cup grated Parmesan cheese

Brown the chicken in the butter, turning to brown evenly. Add ½ cup water, the salt, 2 tablespoons white wine, and the lemon juice. Cover and simmer for about 45 minutes, until tender. Remove chicken and keep warm. Add sherry, remaining white wine,

and lemon rind; simmer. Stir in the cream slowly. Return chicken
to the sauce and heat but do not boil. Put in a casserole, cover
with lemon slices and sprinkle with cheese. Place under the
broiler for 2 or 3 minutes. Makes 4 servings.

*Chicken-Almond Casserole

      1 pound mushrooms, sliced
      2 tablespoons butter *or* margarine
      3 cups diced cooked chicken
      1 can (10½ ounces) cream of mushroom soup
      1 can (10½ ounces) chicken-rice soup
      1 can (6 ounces) evaporated milk
      1 can chow-mein noodles
      1 cup slivered almonds

Sauté the mushrooms in the butter until lightly browned. Add
chicken, soups, evaporated milk and noodles. Turn into a shallow
2-quart baking dish and sprinkle with almonds. Bake in preheated 350° oven about 45 minutes. Makes 6 servings.

Chicken-Cabbage Casserole

      ½ cup flour
      2 teaspoons salt
      ¼ teaspoon pepper
      1 broiler-fryer, 2½ to 3 pounds, cut up
      ¼ cup oil
      1 small onion, sliced
      ¼ teaspoon caraway seed
      1 cup milk
      1 cup chicken broth
      ½ small head cabbage, shredded (about 6 cups)

Mix flour, salt and pepper and coat chicken (reserve excess flour mixture). In large skillet heat oil over medium-high heat and brown chicken on both sides; remove. Sauté onion in fat until golden brown and tender, then stir in caraway seed and reserved flour mixture until smooth. Gradually stir in milk and broth; cook and stir until thickened. Spread cabbage in 13" x 9" x 2" baking dish, pour sauce over and top with chicken. Cover and bake in 375° oven 45 to 50 minutes, or until cabbage is tender. Serves 4 to 6.

Chicken-Macaroni Casserole

    ½ cup chopped onion
    1 tablespoon butter *or* margarine
    1 can (10½ ounces) cream of chicken soup
  1½ cups finely shredded Cheddar cheese
    1 can (13 ounces) boned chicken with broth *or*
    1 pound raw chicken
    ¾ cup chicken broth
    2 hard-cooked eggs, chopped
    2 small tomatoes, quartered
    2 cups (about 8 ounces) elbow macaroni, cooked

In skillet, sauté onion in the butter until golden. Stir in soup and 1 cup cheese until cheese melts. Cut chicken in bite-size pieces and add to soup with broth and last 3 ingredients. Spoon into buttered shallow 1½-quart casserole and sprinkle with remaining cheese. Bake at 350° 30 minutes, or until browned and bubbly. Makes 6 servings.

Green Noodle-Chicken Casserole

> 1 package (8 ounces) green noodles, cooked
> 2 teaspoons salt
> 2 broiler-fryers, 3 pounds *each,* cut up
> ¼ teaspoon pepper
> 3 tablespoons butter
> 1 medium onion, minced
> ¼ cup flour
> ½ teaspoon tarragon
> 1 cup chicken broth
> 1½ cups half-and-half *or* milk

Cook the noodles in deep water with 1 teaspoon salt for 5 minutes only. Drain and put into a casserole. Meanwhile sprinkle the chicken with remaining salt and the pepper and brown in butter. Transfer to the casserole on top of the noodles. (You may want to do the chicken in batches.) Add onion to the drippings and, when light brown, stir in the flour and tarragon until smooth. Pour in the broth and half-and-half, stirring steadily. When smooth and thickened, pour over the casserole, cover and bake at 350° for 45 minutes. Makes 6 servings.

Casserole of Chicken and Prunes

> 2 broiler-fryers, cut up, *or* 16 chicken thighs
> 6 medium onions, sliced thick
> 2 tablespoons flour
> 1½ teaspoons salt
> ¼ teaspoon pepper
> 1 package (12 ounces) pitted prunes
> 2 cans (8 ounces *each*) tomato sauce

If using thighs, bone them. Put half the onions in a greased casserole and sprinkle with half the flour, add half the chicken and sprinkle with half the salt and pepper. Add half the prunes and

1 can of tomato sauce. Repeat. Bake covered at 350° for about 1½ hours. Makes 8 servings.

Chicken with Grapes

> 2 broiler-fryers, about 3 pounds *each*, cut up
> 1 teaspoon salt
> 3 tablespoons butter
> ¼ cup water
> 1 cup white wine
>   Pinch cloves
>   Pinch rosemary
> 1 cup seedless grapes

Sprinkle the chicken with salt and brown in butter, turning to brown on all sides. Add the water and then the wine. Pour into a casserole or ovenproof serving dish, season with cloves and rosemary and salt to taste. Bake at 350° for half an hour. Add the grapes and cook 20 minutes more. Makes 6 servings.

Casserole of Chicken in Soy Sauce

> 1 cup soy sauce
> 1 tablespoon sugar
> 1 teaspoon minced ginger *or* ½ teaspoon powdered
> 1 cup water
> 1 frying chicken, 3 pounds, cut up
> 2 cups cooked rice
>   Watercress (optional)

Combine the soy, sugar, ginger and water. Put the chicken in a casserole, pour over the soy mixture, cover and simmer gently for 45 minutes, until tender. Turn the chicken pieces at least once. Add the rice and spoon the sauce over. Makes 4 servings.

If you wish to serve this cold, omit the rice. Let the chicken cool in the cooking liquid and serve on a bed of watercress. The liquid will be jellied and can be sliced over the chicken.

*Chicken Casserole with Crumb Dumplings

> ¼ cup vegetable oil
> ⅓ cup flour
> ½ teaspoon salt
> ⅛ teaspoon pepper
> 2 cups chicken broth
> 1 can (10 ounces) cream of chicken soup
> 1 can (1 pound) small onions, drained
> 3 cups diced cooked chicken
> Crumb Dumplings (see below)
> Chicken gravy (optional)

In saucepan, blend oil, flour and seasonings. Gradually add broth and cook, stirring, until thickened. Remove from heat and stir in next 3 ingredients. Put in greased 13″ x 9″ x 2″ baking dish and top with dumplings. Bake at 425° 20 to 25 minutes. Serve with gravy, if desired. Makes 6 servings.

Crumb Dumplings

> 2 cups all-purpose flour
> 3 teaspoons baking powder
> ½ teaspoon salt
> 1 teaspoon *each* poultry seasoning, onion flakes and celery seed
> 1 tablespoon poppy seed
> ¼ cup vegetable oil
> 1 cup milk
> 3 tablespoons margarine, melted
> ¾ cup fine dry bread crumbs

Mix dry ingredients, except crumbs, and add oil and milk. Stir just until moistened. Drop by rounded tablespoonfuls into mixture of margarine and crumbs. Roll to coat.

Baked Chicken and Rice

      1 frying chicken, about 3 pounds, cut up
      ¼ cup flour
      1 teaspoon salt
      ¼ teaspoon pepper
      ¼ cup margarine
      2 cups boiling water
      3 chicken bouillon cubes
      1 teaspoon instant minced onion
      1 cup raw rice
        Paprika

Shake chicken pieces in mixture of next 3 ingredients in plastic
bag. Melt margarine in shallow 2-quart baking dish in hot oven
(400°). Put chicken, skin side down, in dish and bake 20 minutes.
Remove chicken and put water in dish with remaining ingredients, except paprika. Mix well and arrange chicken, skin side up,
on top. Put back in oven and bake 40 minutes longer. Sprinkle
with paprika. Makes 4 servings.

Baked Chicken, Beans and Rice

      1 broiler-fryer, about 3 pounds, cut up
      2 tablespoons butter *or* margarine
      1 cup raw rice
      1 package (10 ounces) frozen Italian green beans,
        thawed
      ¾ cup chopped onion
      ¾ teaspoon oregano
      ½ teaspoon basil
      ⅛ teaspoon garlic powder
      ⅛ teaspoon pepper
      3 chicken bouillon cubes
     2½ cups boiling water

Brown chicken in butter in large skillet. Meanwhile combine remaining ingredients in 3-quart casserole. Top with chicken.

Cover and bake at 350° 1 hour, stirring rice once. Uncover and bake 15 minutes longer. Makes 4 servings.

*Scalloped Chicken Casserole

    1½ cups bread crumbs
    ¼ cup butter
    ½ teaspoon thyme
    1 tablespoon grated onion
    ½ teaspoon salt
    ¼ teaspoon pepper
    ¼ cup flour
    2½ cups chicken broth
    2½ to 3 cups diced cooked chicken

Combine the bread crumbs with 2 tablespoons butter and heat for 2 or 3 minutes. Add the next 4 ingredients. In another pan, melt remaining butter, stir in the flour and pour in the broth slowly while stirring. Season with a little salt to taste. Simmer for 2 or 3 minutes, until smooth and thickened. Cool. Put the crumbs, gravy, and chicken in alternate layers into a casserole, ending with crumbs on top. Bake at 350° for 25 minutes. Makes 6 servings.

Baked Coconut Chicken

    ¾ cup packaged grated coconut
    6 tablespoons flour
    1½ teaspoons salt
    Dash of pepper
    ⅛ teaspoon garlic salt
    1 broiler-fryer, about 3 pounds, cut up
    1 egg, slightly beaten
    Fat for frying

Mix first 5 ingredients. Dip chicken pieces in egg, then roll in coconut mixture. Heat about ¼″ fat in heavy skillet. Add chicken and brown on all sides. Remove chicken and put in shallow baking pan or casserole. Bake at 350° about 30 minutes. Serves 4.

Almond Chicken

> ½ cup flour
> 1 teaspoon salt
> ⅛ teaspoon pepper
> 1 teaspoon paprika
> 1 broiler-fryer, about 3 pounds, cut up
> 1 egg, slightly beaten
> 1½ tablespoons milk
> 1 cup finely chopped almonds
> 2 tablespoons butter *or* margarine, melted
> Salt

Mix first 4 ingredients. Add chicken and coat, then dip in combined egg and milk. Coat with almonds and put, skin side down, on lightly oiled foil-lined pan. Drizzle with butter and sprinkle generously with salt. Bake at 375° 20 minutes, turn skin side up and bake 40 minutes longer, or until browned. Makes 4 servings.

Cheesy Cracker-Meal Chicken

> ⅔ cup cracker meal
> ½ teaspoon salt
> 1 broiler-fryer, about 3 pounds, cut up
> ⅓ cup grated Parmesan cheese
> ½ teaspoon paprika
> ¼ cup minced crisp bacon
> 1 egg, beaten
> 3 tablespoons water

Mix cracker meal and salt and coat chicken with mixture. Add next 3 ingredients to remainder and mix well. Dip chicken in egg mixed with water and coat with cracker-meal mixture. Put in lightly oiled foil-lined pan or casserole and bake at 400° 30 minutes. Turn chicken and bake 30 minutes longer, or until well browned. Makes 4 servings.

Double-Cheese Chicken

    ¼ cup flour
    ½ teaspoon salt
    1 broiler-fryer, about 3 pounds, cut up
    1 egg
    1 tablespoon water
    2 tablespoons butter *or* margarine, melted
    1 cup (about 30) crushed cheese crackers
    ½ cup finely shredded Cheddar cheese

Mix flour and salt and coat chicken with mixture. Dip in egg beaten with the water and butter. Coat with mixture of last 2 ingredients. Put in lightly oiled foil-lined pan or casserole and bake at 375° 1 hour, or until well browned. Makes 4 servings.

Potato-Chip-Coated Baked Chicken

    ¼ cup butter *or* margarine
    1½ cups (4½ ounces) finely crushed potato chips
    1 teaspoon salt
    ¼ teaspoon pepper
    Dash of paprika
    1 egg, slightly beaten
    2 tablespoons milk
    1 broiler-fryer, about 3 pounds, cut up

Melt butter in shallow baking pan in moderate oven (375°). Mix chips and seasonings. Beat egg and milk together, dip chicken pieces in the mixture, then coat on both sides with chips. Arrange in baking pan and bake 1 hour, or until well browned and tender. Makes 4 servings.

Baked Orange Chicken

> 1 broiler-fryer, about 3 pounds, cut up
> ¼ cup margarine
> 1 orange, sliced crosswise
> 2 tablespoons flour
> ½ teaspoon salt
> ⅛ teaspoon cinnamon
> 1½ cups orange juice

In large skillet brown chicken in margarine. Arrange with orange slices in 12″ x 8″ x 2″ baking dish. In same skillet blend in flour, salt and cinnamon. Gradually stir in orange juice and cook and stir over medium-high heat until juice thickens and boils. Pour over chicken and orange slices. Bake at 375° 1 hour or until chicken is tender. Makes 4 servings.

Orange-Ginger Chicken

> ¼ cup butter *or* margarine
> 2 tablespoons orange juice
> ½ teaspoon salt
> 1 broiler-fryer, about 3 pounds, cut up
> 1 cup (about 20) crushed gingersnaps
> ¼ cup flour
> 1 tablespoon grated orange rind

Mix first 3 ingredients and brush on chicken; reserve remainder. Mix remaining ingredients and coat chicken with mixture. Put in lightly oiled baking dish and drizzle reserved butter mixture over top. Bake at 375° 1 hour, or until tender. Makes 4 servings.

Spicy Chicken with Oranges

    1 broiler-fryer, about 3 pounds, cut up
    ¼ cup flour
    1 teaspoon salt
    ⅛ teaspoon pepper
    ½ teaspoon cinnamon
    ½ teaspoon ground cloves
    ¼ cup butter
    4 oranges
    1 tablespoon *each* soy sauce and brown sugar

Shake chicken pieces in bag with flour, salt and spices. Heat butter in heavy skillet or Dutch oven, add chicken and brown slowly on all sides. Peel and section oranges, saving all the juice. Measure juice; you need ½ cup. Add juice, soy sauce and brown sugar and pour over chicken. Cover and cook over low heat 25 minutes, or until tender. Add orange sections and heat gently. Makes 4 servings.

Orange-Honey Chicken

    1 cup fine dry bread crumbs
    1 tablespoon grated orange rind
    1 teaspoon salt
    ¼ teaspoon pepper
    1 broiler-fryer, about 3 pounds, cut up
    ½ cup orange juice
    1 chicken bouillon cube
    ½ cup boiling water
    ¼ cup butter
    ½ cup honey

Mix first 4 ingredients. Dip chicken in orange juice and coat with crumb mixture. Put on lightly oiled foil-lined pan or greased casserole and bake at 350° 30 minutes. Meanwhile, dissolve bouillon cube in water and add last 2 ingredients, stirring until butter melts. Pour over chicken and bake, basting frequently, 30 to 40 minutes longer, or until chicken is browned. Makes 4 servings.

Marmalade Baked Chicken

    1 broiler-fryer, about 3 pounds, cut up
      Salt and pepper
    ½ cup orange marmalade
    1 tablespoon *each* vinegar and gravy seasoning-
      and-browning sauce

Wash and dry chicken pieces and arrange in baking pan. Sprinkle with salt and pepper. Bake at 400° 30 minutes. Brush with mixture of remaining ingredients and bake 15 minutes longer. Makes 4 servings.

Wheat-Germ Chicken with Peaches

    ¼ cup flour
    1 teaspoon salt
    ⅛ teaspoon pepper
    1 broiler-fryer, about 3 pounds, cut up
    1 egg, slightly beaten
    3 tablespoons butter *or* margarine, melted
    1 cup toasted plain wheat germ
    1 can (1 pound) peach halves, drained

Mix first 3 ingredients and coat chicken with the mixture. Brush with egg beaten with 2 tablespoons melted butter. Coat with ¾ cup wheat germ. Put on lightly oiled foil-lined pan and bake at

400° 30 minutes. Meanwhile, brush peach halves with remaining butter and coat with remaining wheat germ. Arrange in pan with chicken and bake 30 minutes longer. Makes 4 servings.

Baked Chicken and Sweet Potatoes

> 1 broiler-fryer, about 3 pounds, quartered
> Salt and pepper
> ¼ cup apricot preserves
> ¼ cup packed brown sugar
> 2 teaspoons lemon juice
> 2 tablespoons margarine
> 4 medium sweet potatoes, cooked and peeled

Put chicken in shallow baking dish and sprinkle with salt and pepper. Spread with preserves, then sprinkle with brown sugar. Sprinkle with lemon juice and dot with margarine. Cover tightly and bake in preheated 400° oven 30 minutes. Uncover and add potatoes. Baste with drippings in dish and bake, basting once or twice, 30 minutes longer, or until chicken is well browned and done. Makes 4 servings.

Oniony Chicken

> ⅓ cup flour
> 1 envelope (1⅜ ounces) onion-soup mix
> ½ cup butter *or* margarine, melted
> 1 broiler-fryer, about 3 pounds, cut up
> 1⅓ cups crushed crisp rice cereal, cornflakes *or*
>   wheat cereal

Combine first 2 ingredients until well blended. Stir in butter. Dip chicken in mixture and roll in cereal. Put in lightly oiled baking pan or casserole and bake at 400° 1 hour, or until well browned. Makes 4 servings.

Pretzel Baked Chicken

> 2 broiler-fryers, about 2½ pounds *each*, quartered
> 2 cups finely crushed pretzels (blender can be used)
> 1 teaspoon paprika
> ¼ teaspoon pepper
> ½ teaspoon oregano leaves
> ½ teaspoon poultry seasoning
> ⅔ cup margarine, melted

Wash chicken and pat dry. Mix remaining ingredients, except margarine. Line a shallow baking pan with foil and brush generously with margarine. Brush chicken on both sides with margarine and dip in crumb mixture. Put on baking sheet and bake in moderate oven (350°) 1 hour, or until chicken is tender. Makes 6 servings.

*Baked Chicken Hash Casserole

> 2 cups chopped cooked chicken
> 1 onion, chopped
> 1 green pepper, minced
> 2 pimientos, diced
> 2 carrots, shredded
> Salt
> 2 tablespoons chopped parsley
> ¼ teaspoon poultry seasoning
> 2 cups chicken gravy *or* strong broth

Combine all ingredients and mix thoroughly. Spoon into a casserole. Cover and bake at 350° for an hour. Uncover and bake for about 10 minutes longer. Makes 4 servings.

Cornish Game Hen Casserole

> 3 game hens, about 1½ pounds *each*, split
> ½ cup flour
> 1 teaspoon salt
> ¼ teaspoon pepper
>   Butter for sautéeing
> 1 cup chicken broth
> 1 tablespoon lemon juice
> ½ teaspoon poultry seasoning

Dredge the game hens with flour mixed with salt and pepper. Sauté in butter until golden brown on both sides. Pour into a casserole; add broth, lemon juice and poultry seasoning. Bake, covered, in a preheated oven at 375° for 35 to 40 minutes. If you wish, thicken juices with a little of the seasoned flour made into a paste with a little chicken broth. Makes 6 servings.

7 *Chicken Potpies*

Chicken potpie is an all-American favorite, whether it is made from scratch, using an entire chicken, or from leftover bits and pieces. There are various kinds of topping: biscuit dough, individual biscuits, pie crust, bread, or cornbread. Being a one-dish meal, it saves time and energy, and it can save money as well since vegetables, new or previously cooked, will help to make the chicken go a long way.

Chicken Potpie

    1 roaster, about 5 pounds
    Water
    1 cup chopped celery
    1 medium onion, chopped
    Sprig of parsley
    1 bay leaf
    2 teaspoons salt
    ¼ cup butter
    ¼ cup flour
    Biscuit Dough (see following)

Put the chicken in a large pot with water to cover. Add celery, onion, parsley, bay leaf, and salt. Cover and simmer for about 1½ to 2 hours, until chicken is very tender. Remove and when cool enough to handle take meat from the bones, keeping it in large pieces. Meanwhile, chill the broth enough to bring fat to the top. Skim off as much as possible and strain the broth. Melt the butter, blend in the flour, and pour in 2 to 2½ cups broth while stirring. Cook until smooth and thickened. Reseason to taste with salt and pepper. Put the chicken in a shallow 1½-quart casserole and pour the sauce over. (If there is not enough liquid to cover the meat, add more broth or heavy cream.) Use the recipe for Biscuit Dough or a mix. Cover the casserole with the dough, fit it around the edges and slash the top. Bake at 450° until heated through and the top is light brown, about 20 minutes. Makes 6 servings.

Biscuit Dough

    2 cups flour
    ¾ teaspoon salt
    1 tablespoon baking powder
    6 tablespoons shortening
    2 tablespoons minced parsley
    ¼ teaspoon thyme
    ¾ cup milk

Sift the flour, salt, and baking powder together. Cut in the shortening thoroughly. Add parsley and thyme. Add the milk and stir until blended. Turn onto a floured board and knead briefly. Pat or roll lightly to about ½″ thickness. Cut with a floured biscuit cutter or into squares with a floured knife or make into about a 9″ circle.

Herbed Chicken Pie

> 1 roasting chicken, about 5 pounds
> Celery leaves
> Parsley sprigs
> 3 onions, chopped
> 2 teaspoons salt
> ½ cup flour
> ¼ teaspoon pepper
> ¼ teaspoon marjoram
> ⅛ teaspoon thyme
> ½ teaspoon tarragon *or* chervil
> Biscuit Dough (see page 82 or use mix)

Simmer the chicken in water almost to cover with celery leaves, parsley sprigs, 1 onion, chopped, and 2 teaspoons salt, for about 1½ hours or until almost tender. Remove chicken and when cool enough to handle remove meat from bones. Return the skin and bones to the broth and simmer, covered, for about an hour. Strain, chill, and remove and reserve fat. Cut chicken into serving pieces and place in the bottom of a 3-quart casserole. Sauté the remaining onions in reserved chicken fat until light brown. Add flour and when blended, pour in the chicken broth while stirring. You'll need 3 to 4 cups; augment with canned chicken broth if necessary. Add remaining ingredients except the topping. Reseason. Simmer until thickened and pour over the chicken. Cover the casserole and heat for 30 minutes in the oven at 350°. Make biscuits from Biscuit Dough or use a mix, following package instructions. Space the biscuits over the top. Bake at 425° for about 18 to 20 minutes, until biscuits are light brown and the pie heated through. Makes 6 servings.

*Chicken Vegetable Pie with Crust

 3 tablespoons butter *or* margarine
 ¼ cup flour
 1 cup half-and-half
 1½ cups chicken broth
 ½ teaspoon tarragon
 ½ teaspoon savory
 1 tablespoon minced chives
 2 cups cooked green peas *or* 1 package (10 ounces)
    frozen
 2 cups sliced carrots *or* 1 can (10 ounces) diced
 2½ to 3 cups cubed cooked chicken
    Salt and pepper
    Pastry Topping for Pies (see below)

Melt the butter and stir in the flour until smooth. Pour in the half-and-half and broth slowly while stirring. Add seasonings, vegetables, and chicken and stir. Season with salt and pepper. Pour into a 9″ casserole. Place the pastry on top and crimp the edges. Bake in a preheated oven at 425° for half an hour, until heated through and top crust is light brown. Makes 6 servings.

Pastry Topping for Pie

 ½ cup butter *and/or* shortening
 1 cup flour
 ½ teaspoon salt
    About ¼ cup ice water

Cut the shortening into the flour and salt with a pastry blender or 2 knives, used scissors fashion. The pieces should be a little coarser than cornmeal. Sprinkle in the ice water a tablespoon at a time, tossing lightly with a fork and adding only enough water so pastry will form a ball. Chill and roll out, from center to outside, on a lightly floured board. Form a circle about ¼″ thick and a little larger than the top of the casserole. Fold dough over, place it on the casserole and crimp the edges. Slash to let the steam out.

*Two Crust Potpie

Double recipe Pastry Topping for Pie (see page 84)
2 tablespoons minced onion
1 tablespoon butter
4 cups cut-up cooked chicken
1 tablespoon minced parsley
1 can (1 pound) small white onions, drained
2 cups chicken gravy *or* strong broth
Milk (optional)

Line the bottom and sides of a deep pie plate or shallow casserole with half of the pastry. Sauté the onion in the butter for 2 or 3 minutes and combine with the chicken, parsley, and onions. Stir in the gravy. Fill the casserole and top with remaining crust; crimp the edges and slash the center. Bake at 400° for about half an hour, until heated through and brown on top. For a browner crust, brush it with a little milk before baking. Makes 6 servings.

*Bread-Topped Chicken Pie

1 large onion, minced
4 small carrots, scraped and cut into thin rounds
1 cup chicken broth
1 package (10 ounces) frozen peas *or* 1 cup cooked fresh
3 cups diced cooked chicken
¼ cup soft butter
2 tablespoons flour
½ cup half-and-half *or* cream
6 slices stale white bread

Simmer the onion and carrots in chicken broth for 10 minutes, covered. Add the peas and cook 5 minutes longer. Add the

chicken and pour into a baking dish. Meanwhile melt 2 tablespoons of the butter, blend in the flour, and pour in the half-
and-half slowly while stirring. Simmer gently until smooth and
thickened and stir into the baking dish. Cut the crusts off of the
bread and cut into squares. Toast on one side and butter the
other. Place on top of casserole toasted side down. Bake at 400°
until heated through and bread is lightly browned. Makes 6
servings.

*Dixie Chicken, Ham and Cornbread Potpie

        3 tablespoons butter
        3 tablespoons flour
    2½ cups chicken broth
        2 cups diced cooked chicken
        2 cups diced cooked ham
        1 teaspoon salt
    ¼ teaspoon pepper
        Cornbread Batter (see below)

Melt the butter and blend in the flour. Gradually add the
chicken broth. Stir until thickened. Add the diced chicken and
ham. Season with salt and pepper. Pour into a shallow casserole
about 9″ in diameter. Spread cornbread batter over the top of
the meat and gravy. Bake at 400° for 20 to 25 minutes, until
the cornbread is brown. Makes 6 servings.

Cornbread Batter

        1 egg
        1 teaspoon sugar
    ⅓ cup milk
    ¼ cup melted shortening *or* salad oil
    ⅔ cup flour
    ⅓ cup cornmeal
    1½ teaspoons baking powder
    ¼ teaspoon salt

Beat the egg lightly; add sugar, milk and shortening. Sift together the remaining ingredients. Add liquids to the cornmeal mixture all at once. Blend together with as few strokes as possible.

*Chicken Pie with Crumbs and Cheese

       4 slices bread, cubed
       3 tablespoons butter *or* margarine
       3 cups diced cooked chicken
    1½ cups Cream Sauce (see below)
       ¼ cup tomato catsup
          Bread crumbs
          Grated cheese

Fry the bread cubes in butter until golden on all sides. Put in the bottom of a 10" pie plate and spread the chicken over the bread. Mix the cream sauce with catsup and pour over. Top with bread crumbs and cheese. Bake at 350° about 20 minutes, until hot and light brown on top. Makes 6 servings.

Cream Sauce

       3 tablespoons butter
       3 tablespoons flour
    1¼ cups hot milk

Melt the butter and stir in the flour over low heat. When blended, add the milk slowly while stirring. Continue to stir and cook for several minutes. Yield: about 1½ cups.

*Potato-Topped Chicken Pie

> 2 cups mashed potatoes (homemade or instant)
> ¼ cup grated cheese
> 3 cups diced cooked chicken
> 1 cup leftover cooked vegetables
> 2 tablespoons chicken gravy *or* broth
> 2 tablespoons melted butter
> Dry bread crumbs

Mix the mashed potatoes with 2 tablespoons grated cheese. Combine the chicken, vegetables, and gravy or broth in a small baking dish. Spoon the potatoes over the top. Pour over the melted butter and sprinkle with a few bread crumbs mixed with remaining cheese. Bake until heated through and top is lightly browned. Makes 4 servings.

Chicken Noodle Potpie

> 1 chicken, about 5 pounds, cut up
> 2 teaspoons salt
> Water
> 8 ounces medium-wide noodles
> ¼ cup butter *or* chicken fat
> ¼ cup flour
> ½ cup white wine
> ½ cup heavy cream
> ½ cup diced celery
> ¼ cup diced onion
> Pastry Topping for Pie (see page 84)

Put the chicken in a pot with the salt; add water almost to cover. Simmer covered for 1½ hours or until chicken is tender. Take out the chicken and when cool enough to handle remove meat from the bones and cut into serving-size pieces. Return the skin and bones to the pot and simmer half an hour. Pour off 1 cup broth and set aside. Cook the noodles in remaining broth for 15 minutes. Drain. Meanwhile, melt the butter, blend in the flour and pour in the chicken broth, wine and cream, while stirring. Add the celery and onions and simmer 10 minutes. Put the noodles and chicken in a buttered 2½-quart baking dish 9″ in diameter. Pour the sauce over. Place the pastry on top and crimp the edges over the edge of the dish. Slash the pastry with a "V" in the center. Bake in a preheated oven at 425° half an hour. Makes 6 servings.

8 *Fruited Birds*

Chicken and fruit complement each other to perfection. Lemon is a favorite ingredient, but try some others, substituting fruits of your choice for those indicated in the recipes that follow.

Lemon Chicken with Chick-Peas

    1 roasting chicken, 4 to 5 pounds
      Juice of 3 lemons
  ½ cup minced onion
    2 tablespoons olive oil
    2 cups chicken broth
    2 cans (1 pound *each*) chick-peas
    2 cloves garlic, crushed
    1 teaspoon salt
  ½ teaspoon pepper

Rub the chicken inside and out with lemon juice. Sauté the onion in oil for 2 minutes. Add the whole chicken and brown it. Add broth, drained chick-peas, remaining lemon juice, garlic, salt and pepper. Cover and simmer about an hour, until the chicken is tender. Adjust seasoning and serve the bird on a warm platter surrounded by chick-peas. Pour the pan juices over. Makes 6 servings.

Citrus Chicken

    2 broiler-fryers, 2½ to 3 pounds *each*, quartered
    ¼ cup flour
    1 teaspoon salt
    ¼ teaspoon pepper
      Pinch sugar
    ½ cup butter
    1 large grapefruit
    2 or 3 oranges
    ¼ cup juice from the grapefruit *and/or* oranges
      Juice of ½ lemon
    1 cup chicken broth
    ½ cup sherry

Dust the chicken or shake in a paper bag with a mixture of the flour, salt and pepper, sugar; reserve any excess. Sauté the chicken in butter for 15 minutes, turning to brown evenly. Section the grapefruit and oranges, saving any juice; squeeze some, if necessary, to make ¼ cup. Add half the fruit juices and half the broth and simmer covered for half an hour, until chicken is tender and liquid reduced. Remove chicken to a heated platter and keep warm. Add about 2 tablespoons of reserved flour to pan. Stir well, add remaining broth and remaining fruit juices. Boil to thicken and reduce. Add the grapefruit and orange sections and the sherry, heat and pour over the chicken. Makes 6 servings.

Steamed Lemon Chicken

    ½ cup butter
      Juice of 1 lemon
    ¼ cup water
      1 teaspoon salt
      1 clove garlic
      Dash of pepper
    ½ teaspoon paprika
      1 broiler-fryer, about 3 pounds, cut up

Put all ingredients except chicken in skillet and heat. Arrange chicken pieces on rack in skillet. Cover tightly and steam over low heat for 45 minutes, or until tender, turning several times. Makes 4 servings.

Cherry Chicken

      1 broiler-fryer, 2½ to 3 pounds, cut up
        Salt and pepper
        Flour
      2 tablespoons butter *or* margarine
      1 can (1 pound) water-packed pitted red sour
          cherries
    ⅓ cup sugar

Season chicken with salt and pepper, roll in flour and brown in the butter in skillet. Cover and sauté gently 35 minutes, or until tender. Remove from skillet and pour off fat, leaving about 1 tablespoon in pan. Stir in 1 tablespoon flour. Add cherries and liquid and the sugar and cook, stirring gently, until thickened. Put chicken in skillet and simmer a few minutes. Good with rice. Makes 4 servings.

Potted Chicken with Vegetables

> 1 broiler-fryer, 3 to 3½ pounds, cut up
> ¼ cup flour
>   Salt
> ½ teaspoon paprika
> ⅛ teaspoon pepper
> 2 tablespoons margarine
> 2 cups water
> ½ teaspoon rosemary, crumbled
> ¼ teaspoon marjoram, crumbled
> 2 cups carrots, cut in strips about 2" x ½"
> 2 teaspoons lemon juice
> 1 package (10 ounces) frozen green peas
> 1 package (12 ounces) frozen French-fried potatoes

Dip chicken pieces in mixture of flour, 1 teaspoon salt, the paprika and pepper. Brown in the margarine in large heavy kettle or Dutch oven. Add 1 cup water, the rosemary and marjoram. Cover and simmer about 35 minutes, then add carrots, lemon juice and remaining water. Cover and simmer 20 minutes, or until chicken and carrots are tender. Add peas and French fries and sprinkle with salt. Simmer 10 minutes longer, or until potatoes are hot. Makes 4 to 6 servings.

Chicken with Grapes in Sherry

> 1 broiler-fryer, about 3 pounds, cut up
> 2 tablespoons flour
> 1 teaspoon salt
> ⅛ teaspoon pepper
> ¼ cup slivered blanched almonds
> 3 tablespoons olive oil
> 1 small onion, chopped
> 1 cup diced celery
> 1 small clove garlic, minced
> 1 cup seedless grapes
>   Chopped parsley
> ¾ cup dry sherry

Dredge chicken pieces with mixture of flour and seasonings. Brown almonds lightly in oil in skillet or Dutch oven. Remove almonds and brown chicken pieces on all sides in oil remaining in skillet. Remove chicken pieces and add next 4 ingredients and 2 tablespoons parsley to skillet. Cook 2 to 3 minutes. Add sherry and bring to boil. Add chicken, cover and simmer about 45 minutes. Remove to serving dish; sprinkle with almonds and parsley. Makes 4 servings.

Holiday Chicken

> 1 broiler-fryer, about 3 pounds, cut up
> 1 cup canned eggnog *or* 1 egg beaten with ¾ cup milk
> ⅔ cup *each* flour and ground pecans
> 2 teaspoons salt
>   Butter *or* margarine
> 1 cup water
> ½ cup orange juice
> ¾ cup mixed diced candied fruit

Dip chicken in eggnog. Put flour, nuts and salt in paper or plastic bag, add 2 pieces chicken at a time and shake until well coated. Brown slowly on all sides in butter in skillet. Pour off excess fat and add the water and orange juice. Reduce heat, cover and simmer 25 minutes. Add fruit, cover and simmer 20 minutes longer, or until chicken is tender. Good with rice. Makes 4 servings.

Tarragon Chicken

      1 broiler-fryer, about 3 pounds, cut up
  1¼ teaspoons salt
   ¼ teaspoon pepper
      2 tablespoons vegetable oil
      1 can (16 ounces) tomatoes
      2 tablespoons orange juice
   ½ pound fresh mushrooms, sliced, *or* 2 cans (3
            ounces *each*) chopped mushrooms, drained
   ¼ pound cooked ham, diced
   ¼ cup dry white wine
      1 small green pepper, chopped
      2 teaspoons instant minced onion
  1¼ teaspoons dried tarragon, crumbled, *or* 1 tablespoon
            fresh
      2 tablespoons flour
         Hot cooked rice

Sprinkle chicken with the salt and pepper and brown on all sides in hot oil in large skillet. Add remaining ingredients, except last 2, bring to boil, cover and simmer 45 minutes, or until chicken is tender. Remove chicken to hot serving dish. Stir in flour blended with small amount of cold water and cook, stirring, until thickened. Pour over chicken and serve with rice. Makes 4 servings.

Sesame Chicken with Rice

    1 broiler-fryer, about 3 pounds, cut up
    2 tablespoons vegetable oil
    1 tablespoon sesame seed
    ¼ cup sugar
    2 tablespoons cornstarch
    ⅛ teaspoon ginger
    1 cup water
    1 can (8¼ ounces) crushed pineapple
    ⅓ cup soy sauce
    1 clove garlic, crushed
      Hot cooked rice

Brown chicken pieces on both sides in the oil in large skillet.
Remove chicken and brown seed lightly in the skillet. Remove
from heat, add next 3 ingredients and mix well. Stir in next 4
ingredients. Cook, stirring, until thickened. Add chicken, cover
and simmer 45 minutes, or until tender. Serve on rice. Makes 4
servings.

Chicken in a Bag

    1 broiler-fryer, about 3 pounds
    1 lemon, quartered
    1 onion, halved or quartered
    1 rib celery, cut in 2″ chunks
      Parsley sprig
    1 tablespoon butter or margarine, melted
      Seasoned salt
      Grated rind of 1 orange
    4 potatoes, peeled and halved
    4 carrots, scraped and halved crosswise

Stuff cavity of chicken with next 4 ingredients. Rub outside of chicken with the butter and sprinkle with seasoned salt and orange rind. Put in cooking bag with vegetables. Secure bag and puncture. Put in baking pan and roast in preheated oven at 400° 1¼ hours. Makes 4 servings.

9 *Outdoor Cooking*

Almost every outdoor chef has discovered that the fire is inclined to reach perfection shortly *after* the meal is finished. To avoid this, start at least 45 minutes ahead of time; the coals—usually briquettes—should be gray on the edges and glowing inside.

When cooking a whole chicken on a spit, it should be trussed, keeping the wings and legs close to the body, and the neck, if long, skewered to the back. Thrust the rod in at the tail and out at the wishbone. Roast for about 2 hours; on an electric spit, 1½ hours should be enough, but check with the manufacturer's instructions. A whole chicken may also be cooked on a grill, in which case it must be turned often to ensure even cooking. Whether using a spit or grill, baste frequently with a marinade, wine or butter; however, if using a tomato-base sauce, or one made with sugar, baste for the last 20 minutes only, since the sauce will darken and burn. Chicken parts broiled on a spit or grill will be done in about ⅓ less time than a whole bird. A covered grill will cook more evenly and quickly than an open one; fortunately, an open grill can be easily converted into a covered one by means of layers of foil.

If you are short of time, or have a large number of guests and a small grilling area, the chickens will taste just as good if you partially cook them ahead of time and brown them outdoors for the last 20 minutes. Your guests will be amazed at the speed with which the delicious chickens have been produced!

Barbecued Chicken I

½ cup margarine, softened
1 tablespoon prepared mustard
½ teaspoon salt
2 teaspoons paprika
2 teaspoons vinegar
2 broiler-fryers, 2 to 2½ pounds *each,* split

Mix first 5 ingredients thoroughly. Arrange chicken halves, skin side down, on rack of broiler pan. Spread with half the mixture and broil slowly about 25 minutes. Turn and spread with remaining mixture. Broil 25 minutes. Makes 4 servings.

Barbecued Chicken II

1 broiler-fryer, about 3 pounds, cut up
½ cup bottled Italian dressing
½ cup leftover coffee *or* prepared instant coffee
½ cup chili sauce

Arrange chicken pieces in shallow baking pan. Mix remaining ingredients and brush some on chicken. Bake at 350°, basting with remaining sauce every 15 minutes or so, about 1½ hours. Makes 4 servings.

Barbecued Marinated Chicken Wings

> 2 cups of barbecue sauce of your choice, *or*
>   1 cup tomato puree
>   ¼ cup vinegar
>   ¼ cup sugar
>   1 teaspoon salt
>   ¼ teaspoon pepper
>   1 tablespoon prepared mustard
>   1 tablespoon Worcestershire sauce
>   2 cloves garlic, crushed or minced
> 2 pounds chicken wings

Use 2 cups of a barbecue sauce of your choice or combine all of the other ingredients except the wings and mix thoroughly. Marinate the chicken wings for 2 hours. Broil the wings over coals for 15 minutes, brush with the sauce, turn, brush again and cook 15 minutes more. (This may be done in a preheated broiler.) Brush with sauce just before serving and pass any remaining sauce, heated. Makes 4 servings.

Barbecue Sauce Ranchero

> 1 cup *each* vegetable oil and chili sauce
> 2 tablespoons Worcestershire sauce
>   Juice of 2 lemons
> 1 teaspoon monosodium glutamate
> 1 tablespoon sugar
> ½ teaspoon dry mustard
> ¼ teaspoon hot pepper sauce
> 1 small onion, minced
> 1 clove garlic, minced (optional)

Mix all ingredients. Makes about 2⅓ cups, or enough for 4 broiler-fryers.

White-Wine Barbecue Sauce

    1 small onion, minced
    1 clove garlic, minced
    2 tablespoons olive oil
    ½ teaspoon *each* rosemary and paprika
      Salt and pepper to taste
    2 tablespoons chopped parsley
    ¾ cup dry white wine

Sauté onion and garlic lightly in the olive oil in small saucepan. Add remaining ingredients and simmer a few minutes. Makes about ¾ cup, or enough for 2 broiler-fryers.

Orange Barbecue Sauce

    1 can (6 ounces) frozen orange-juice concentrate,
      thawed but undiluted
    2 tablespoons soy sauce
    1 teaspoon instant minced onion
    ½ teaspoon *each* salt and celery seed
    ¼ teaspoon ginger
    ¼ teaspoon hot pepper sauce

Mix all ingredients. Makes about ¾ cup, or enough for 2 broiler-fryers.

Sherry-Currant Barbecue Sauce

    ¼ cup butter *or* margarine
    3 tablespoons minced parsley
    1 chicken bouillon cube
      Thyme *and* basil to taste
    1 teaspoon dry mustard
    1 tablespoon red-currant jelly
    ¼ cup dry sherry

Put all ingredients in small saucepan and heat, stirring, long enough to melt butter and bouillon cube. Makes about ½ cup, or enough for 2 broiler-fryers.

Tomato-Orange Barbecue Sauce

> 1 can (6 ounces) frozen orange-juice concentrate, thawed but undiluted
> 1 can (8 ounces) tomato sauce
> 1 tablespoon soy sauce
> ½ teaspoon *each* ginger and salt

Mix all ingredients and brush on chicken during last 20 to 30 minutes of broiling time. Makes about 1¾ cups, or enough for 3 broiler-fryers.

Spicy Orange Barbecue Sauce

> 1 can (6 ounces) frozen orange-juice concentrate, thawed but undiluted
> 1 juice-can water
> 1 tablespoon prepared mustard
> ½ teaspoon hot pepper sauce
> ¼ cup packed brown sugar
> ½ cup vegetable oil

Mix all ingredients in small saucepan and bring to boil, stirring, over medium heat. Makes about 2 cups, or enough for 3 broiler-fryers.

Herb Barbecue Sauce

⅔ cup vegetable oil
½ cup lemon juice *or* vinegar
2 teaspoons salt
1 teaspoon sugar
1 teaspoon paprika
2 teaspoons tarragon
½ teaspoon *each* basil and marjoram

Mix all ingredients. Makes about 1¼ cups, or enough for 3 broiler-fryers.

Hawaiian Barbecue Sauce

½ cup vegetable oil
¾ cup pineapple juice
¼ cup molasses
¼ cup lemon juice
⅓ cup soy sauce
1 teaspoon ginger

Mix all ingredients in saucepan and simmer 5 minutes. Makes about 2 cups, or enough for 3 broiler-fryers.

Kumquat Barbecue Sauce

2 tablespoons dry mustard
   Dry white wine
6 preserved kumquats, minced fine
1 tablespoon kumquat-preserving syrup
2 to 3 tablespoons soy sauce

Mix mustard with enough white wine to make a fairly thick paste. Add remaining ingredients, mix well and serve on charcoal-broiled chicken. Makes about ¾ cup, enough for 1 broiler-fryer.

Barbecue Quickies

• Melt ½ cup butter *or* margarine and add 2 tablespoons lemon juice, 1 minced clove garlic and ½ cup chopped parsley. Makes about ⅔ cup.

• Mix 3 tablespoons *each* prepared mustard, catsup and vegetable oil. Add 1½ tablespoons soy sauce and 2 tablespoons lemon juice. Makes ⅔ cup.

• Melt ½ cup butter *or* margarine. Add 1 teaspoon crushed rosemary, ¼ teaspoon paprika and juice of 1 lemon. Makes about ⅔ cup.

• Blend ½ cup *each* molasses and prepared mustard. Stir in ½ cup *each* cider vinegar and catsup. Makes about 2 cups.

Camp Chicken

    1 broiler-fryer, about 3 pounds, cut up
      Flour
    1 clove garlic, crushed
    3 tablespoons margarine
    1 can (13 ounces) cream of chicken soup
    1 soup-can water
 1½ cups raw rice
    1 bunch green onions, sliced
    1 can (4 ounces) pimientos, cut in strips
    1 can (5 ounces) water chestnuts, drained
      Soy sauce

Dredge chicken pieces with flour and brown with garlic in the margarine. Add next 3 ingredients. Bring to boil, cover and simmer 45 minutes, or until chicken is tender. Add next 3 ingredients and about ¼ cup soy sauce. Keep covered until the campers gather around and then reheat thoroughly and serve with additional soy sauce. Makes 4 servings.

Charcoal-Broiled Chicken Legs with Herb-Wine Sauce

    ¼ cup vegetable oil
    ½ cup white wine
    1 clove garlic, crushed
    1 teaspoon instant minced onion
    ½ teaspoon *each* salt, celery salt and coarse black
        pepper
    ¼ teaspoon *each* thyme, oregano and rosemary
   12 chicken legs

Mix all ingredients, except chicken. Chill several hours. Arrange chicken legs in shallow pan, mix sauce well and pour over chicken. Cover and chill, turning pieces at least once, about 3 hours. Then drain sauce into small pan. Cover each leg bone with a doubled piece of heavy-duty foil. Grill chicken over charcoal, turning often and basting with sauce, 30 minutes, or until well done. Makes 6 servings.

PART II

Recipes for Parts

10 Breasts

Some of the most interesting and impressive dishes that have been created use only the breasts of chicken. Recognizing this fact, the French call them *Suprêmes de volailles;* we follow suit with several American recipes called "supreme" which feature chicken breasts. Breasts can be purchased whole, split or boned, and can be flattened into cutlets or cut up. There is no limit to the ways in which they can be cooked: they may be roasted, grilled, poached, simmered, fried, sautéed, broiled, cooked in a casserole or in foil, and served in a rainbow of sauces from wine to lemon to cream.

Buying ready-boned chicken breasts (cutlets) adds quite a bit to the price. You can bone them easily yourself and provide the base for many elegant chicken dishes.

Use whole breasts weighing about 1 pound. (From each 1 pound of breast you will have about 6 ounces of bone and 2 of skin. These can be used in making broth.) For boning, use a sharp knife with a 6″ blade. The thinner and sharper the blade, the better for boning.

1. Put chicken breast, skin side down, on cutting board. With knife, cut just through white gristle at neck end of keel bone

(dark bone at center of breast). Bend back and press flat with hands to expose keel bone.

2. Loosen keel bone by running tip of index finger around both sides. Remove bone in one or two pieces.

3. Working with one side of breast, insert tip of knife under long rib bone. Work knife underneath bone and cut free from meat. Lifting bone away from breast, cut meat from rib cage,

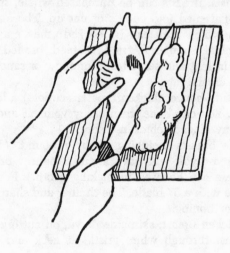

cutting around outer edge of breast up to shoulder joint and then through joint. (This removes entire rib cage.) Turn breast around and repeat process on other side.

4. Working from ends of wishbone, scrape flesh away from each piece of bone. Cut out bone.

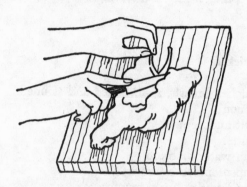

5. Slip knife underneath white tendons on either side of breast to loosen and pull out.

6. Remove skin, if desired.

Chicken Breasts with Herbs

 3 large whole chicken breasts
  Water
 ½ pound mushrooms, sliced
 3 tablespoons butter
 ½ teaspoon tarragon
 2 teaspoons chopped fresh dill
 1 tablespoon minced parsley
 1 teaspoon salt
 ¼ teaspoon pepper
 1 can (10½ ounces) cream of chicken soup
 1 can (10½ ounces) cream of mushroom soup
  Rice, noodles *or* mashed potatoes

Cook the chicken in water just to cover for about 45 minutes, until tender. Reserve broth. Cut meat into bite-size pieces. Sauté the mushrooms in butter for 3 minutes. Add the chicken. Sprinkle with herbs, salt and pepper. Add the soups and 1 cup of the reserved broth. Heat thoroughly. Serve with or over rice, noodles or mashed potatoes. Makes 6 servings.

Mustard Chicken

   2 chicken breasts, split, boned and skinned
   ½ lemon
     Salt and pepper
     Butter
   ¼ cup water *or* broth
   ¼ cup prepared mustard
   ½ cup fine dry bread crumbs

Rub chicken with cut lemon, blot lightly, then season with salt and pepper. Brush lightly with soft butter and place, skin up, in shallow broiler-proof pan. Roast in preheated 425° oven, basting twice with water or broth, 20 to 25 minutes, or until just tender. Cool slightly, then spread with mustard. With fingers, press a layer of crumbs evenly over chicken and put back in baking pan. Drizzle with 2 tablespoons melted butter. Broil low, at least 6″ from heat, until crumbs are crisp and golden brown. Watch carefully that crumbs do not burn. Good warm or cold. Makes 4 servings.

Chicken Breasts in White Wine

3 chicken breasts, split and boned
2 tablespoons olive oil
2 tablespoons butter
¼ cup water
1 teaspoon salt
1 pound mushrooms, sliced
3 tablespoons flour
1 cup white wine
Pinch sugar

Sauté the breasts in a mixture of oil and butter for 20 minutes, turning frequently. Add 2 tablespoons water and salt, cover and cook 10 minutes. Add the mushrooms and stir and cook 5 minutes. Remove chicken and mushrooms and keep warm. Add flour to the drippings and brown while stirring. Pour in the remaining 2 tablespoons water, the wine and sugar. Cook and stir a few minutes and pour over the chicken and mushrooms. Makes 6 servings.

Chicken Breasts with Cheese

2 chicken breasts, boned and skinned
1 egg beaten with 1 tablespoon water
¾ cup seasoned bread crumbs
¼ cup butter *or* part peanut oil
1 can or jar (15 ounces) spaghetti sauce
½ pound mozzarella cheese, shredded
8 to 12 ounces cooked spaghetti *or* spaghettini

Cut the breasts into thin slices. Dip each piece in egg-water mixture and coat with bread crumbs on both sides. Sauté in butter until brown. Put part of the sauce in a baking pan, cover with chicken and top with remaining sauce. Bake at 350° for 20 minutes. When bubbly, add the cheese and bake uncovered until cheese melts. Serve with spaghetti. Makes 4 to 6 servings.

Chicken Breasts Gruyère

    2 whole chicken breasts, about 1 pound *each*
      Salt and pepper
    3 tablespoons butter
    2 tablespoons flour
 1¼ cups milk
    ¼ pound Gruyère cheese, finely shredded
        (about 1 cup)

Split, skin and bone breasts. Sprinkle with salt and pepper and sauté in skillet in 1 tablespoon melted butter 10 minutes, or until done. Remove to broiler-proof platter. Melt remaining butter in skillet and stir in flour. Slowly stir in milk and simmer about 5 minutes. Stir in cheese until melted. Add additional salt to taste. Spoon over chicken (sauce will be very thick). Broil until browned and bubbly. Serve at once. Makes 4 servings.

Chicken Breasts with Beans and
Cheddar-Cheese Sauce

    3 whole chicken breasts, about 1 pound *each*
    1 tablespoon butter *or* margarine
    2 packages (10 ounces *each*) frozen whole green beans
    1 can (10½ ounces) Cheddar-cheese soup
      Dash of cayenne
    ⅓ cup soft bread crumbs
    6 slices bacon, cooked and crumbled
    ½ cup finely shredded Cheddar cheese

Split, skin and bone breasts. Sauté, turning, in the butter in skillet, until browned and tender. Meanwhile, prepare beans as directed on package. Arrange beans in bottom of broiler-proof baking dish. Place cooked chicken on beans. Season soup with cayenne and pour over chicken. Sprinkle with bread crumbs and bacon, combined, and top with cheese. Broil until browned and bubbly. Serve at once. Makes 6 servings.

Chicken Breasts Piedmont Style

    2 whole chicken breasts, boned and split
    2 tablespoons flour
    1 teaspoon salt
    ½ teaspoon white pepper
    2 tablespoons butter *or* margarine
    8 mushrooms, sliced and sautéed
    4 very thin slices Swiss cheese

Put chicken between sheets of waxed paper and roll thin with rolling pin. Coat with flour mixed with the salt and pepper, then cook in the butter 5 to 6 minutes on each side. Put in shallow baking pan; arrange mushroom slices on each breast and cover with cheese. Broil just long enough to melt cheese. Makes 4 servings.

Chicken-Ham Rolls in Cheese Sauce

    2 whole chicken breasts, totaling about 2 pounds
    ¼ cup butter *or* margarine
    16 thin slices boiled ham (½ to ¾ pound)
    2 tablespoons flour
    1 cup milk
    ½ cup shredded sharp Cheddar cheese
    ⅓ cup dry white wine
      Chopped parsley

Split breasts. Remove skin and bones from chicken without breaking meat. Sauté in 2 tablespoons butter in skillet 6 minutes on each side, or until golden; cool. Then cut each half-breast into 4 fingers. Put one in each ham slice, roll up and arrange in shallow 2-quart baking dish. Melt remaining butter in same skillet. Blend in flour. Add milk and cook, stirring, until smooth and thickened. Stir in cheese, then remove from heat and add wine. Pour over rolls and bake in preheated 350° oven 30 minutes. Sprinkle with parsley. Makes 6 servings.

Chicken Breasts in Foil Packages

      3 large whole chicken breasts, split
    1½ cups chicken broth
     ¼ cup flour
     ¼ cup plus 1 tablespoon butter
    1½ cups milk
      2 tablespoons *each* minced scallions, minced celery
        and minced parsley
      1 teaspoon salt
     ¼ teaspoon pepper
     ¼ teaspoon tarragon *or* chervil
        Dash grated nutmeg
     ¼ pound mushrooms, chopped

Simmer the breasts in broth for about 40 minutes, until tender. Remove breasts, reserving broth. When cool enough to handle, pull meat off the bones. Meanwhile, blend the flour into ¼ cup of melted butter. Pour in the milk and ½ cup of the chicken broth slowly while stirring. Add the scallions, celery, parsley, salt, pepper, tarragon and nutmeg. Simmer 5 minutes, stirring from time to time, until smooth and thickened. Sauté the mushrooms in remaining butter and stir into the sauce. Place each piece of chicken on a square of foil. Pour some sauce over each, using it all. Fold the foil in from the sides and then turn it up, folding it envelope fashion. Be sure it is tight so the liquid won't leak out. Place in the oven at 400° for 15 to 20 minutes. Serve in the foil. Makes 6 servings.

Chicken Breasts with Wine and Mushrooms

>   2 whole chicken breasts
> ¼ cup butter *or* margarine
>   1 green onion, minced
> ¼ pound mushrooms, sliced
> ¼ cup chicken broth *or* bouillon
> ¼ cup dry white wine
>   1 cup heavy cream
>   Salt and pepper
>   Lemon juice
>   Chopped parsley

Bone and skin chicken breasts. Sauté breasts in the butter in skillet 6 to 8 minutes, or until flesh is opaque and springs back when pressed lightly with finger. (Do not overcook.) Remove to hot platter and keep warm. Add onion and mushrooms to drippings in skillet and sauté about 5 minutes. Add broth and wine and cook down until syrupy. Add cream and cook until slightly thickened. Season to taste with salt, pepper and lemon juice. Pour over breasts and sprinkle with parsley. Makes 4 servings.

Chicken and Mushrooms in Sour Cream

>   2 tablespoons butter
>   2 tablespoons vegetable *or* olive oil
>   3 large chicken breasts, split
>   2 tablespoons grated onion
>   1 pound mushrooms, cut up
>   1 can (10½ ounces) cream of chicken *or* cream of
>   mushroom soup
> ½ cup chicken broth, heated
> 1½ cups sour cream
>   Salt, pepper and paprika

Melt the butter, blend with oil and sauté the chicken, turning to brown evenly. Add the onion and mushrooms and sauté 5 minutes. Put chicken, vegetables and drippings in a casserole and pour the soup over. Combine the broth with sour cream and pour over all. Season with salt, pepper and paprika to taste. Cover and bake at 350° for 45 minutes. Makes 6 servings.

Chicken Piquant with Yogurt

2 whole chicken breasts, split
4 chicken thighs
  Seasoned flour
¼ cup butter *or* margarine
1 medium onion, chopped
2 cloves garlic, crushed
6 large mushrooms, washed and sliced
¾ cup sauterne
  Salt and pepper
2 to 3 tablespoons cornstarch
1½ cups plain yogurt

Wash chicken pieces, dry and roll in seasoned flour. Melt butter in Dutch oven or heavy skillet, add chicken and brown on all sides. Add next 4 ingredients and season to taste. Cover and simmer 1 hour, or until chicken is tender. Remove chicken to a hot platter. Thicken liquid with cornstarch blended with a small amount of cold water. Add yogurt and heat gently. Pour over chicken. Makes 4 to 6 servings.

Chilled Chicken with Yogurt

    3 chicken breasts, split
    1 teaspoon salt
    ¼ teaspoon pepper
    2 sprigs parsley
    2 slices lemon *or* lime
    3 thin slices onion
    2 tablespoons white wine
    1 cup yogurt
    ¼ cup sour cream
    2 teaspoons curry powder
    ½ teaspoon salt *or* 1 teaspoon soy sauce
    ¼ cup chopped chutney

Place the chicken on a large piece of foil. Season with salt and pepper and place parsley, lemon, and onion on the chicken. Add the wine and fold the foil so no moisture will escape. Bake at 350° for about an hour. Remove, cool and refrigerate, reserving the liquid. Make sauce by combining the yogurt with sour cream, curry, salt and chutney. Thin with a little liquid from the chicken. Spoon the sauce over the chicken breasts which have been taken from foil and placed on a cold platter. Makes 6 servings.

Julienne Chicken and Eggplant

    2 medium eggplants, peeled and cut into ¼″-thick
       slices
    3 large boneless chicken breasts
    2 tablespoons *each* dry sherry, soy sauce and cornstarch
    ¼ cup oil *or* butter *or* mixture of both
    1 to 2 teaspoons freshly grated ginger
    2 cloves garlic, crushed
    ¾ cup chicken broth

Cut the eggplant into matchlike pieces; cut the chicken into similar strips. Combine the sherry, soy and cornstarch and pour over the chicken. Let stand half an hour. Sauté the chicken in oil and/or butter for 3 minutes. Add eggplant, ginger, garlic and broth. Bring to a boil and simmer 3 minutes. Makes 6 servings.

Baked Chicken with Coconut

> 2 chicken breasts, split
> 3 tablespoons oil
> 2 tablespoons bread crumbs
> 3 tablespoons grated coconut
> 1 teaspoon salt
> ½ teaspoon curry powder
> 2 tablespoons butter *or* margarine

Rub the chicken with oil, using 1 to 1½ tablespoons. Combine the crumbs, coconut, salt and curry, and dip the chicken in the mixture, coating all sides. Melt the butter in a baking dish, add remaining oil, and put in the chicken. Bake, covered, for half an hour in preheated oven at 350°. Remove cover and bake 15 minutes. Makes 4 servings.

Orange-Herb Chicken

> 1½ pounds boned chicken breasts
>   Salt, pepper and monosodium glutamate
> 1 tablespoon grated orange rind
> 1 cup orange juice
> ¼ cup lemon juice
> 1 tablespoon cornstarch
> ½ teaspoon caraway seed
> ¼ teaspoon *each* marjoram and rosemary

Cut chicken in 8 slices and put in shallow baking dish. Sprinkle with salt, pepper and monosodium glutamate. Mix next 4 ingredients in saucepan, stirring until smooth. Add remaining ingredients and cook, stirring, until thickened. Pour over chicken. Bake at 350° for 30 minutes. Makes 4 servings.

Chicken with Lemon Cream Sauce and Rice

    3 whole chicken breasts
    ½ cup flour
    2 teaspoons salt
    2 teaspoons paprika
      Lemon Cream Sauce (see below)
    1 cup raw rice
      Water and salt for cooking rice
      Fat for frying
    ½ cup milk
      Chopped parsley

Bone and skin chicken breasts. Cut meat into ½" strips. Mix next 3 ingredients. (Chicken cooks in only a few minutes, so prepare sauce at this point and keep warm.) Put rice on to cook. Heat ½" fat in large skillet. Dip chicken in the milk, then roll in seasoned flour. Put in hot fat and fry until golden brown and opaque. Scoop out with perforated spoon as it browns and keep hot. Mound rice on large hot platter and pour sauce over top. Put chicken strips in center and sprinkle with parsley. Makes 6 servings.

Lemon Cream Sauce

    ¼ cup butter *or* margarine
    ¼ cup flour
    1 teaspoon salt
    ¼ teaspoon paprika
    1½ cups water
    2 chicken bouillon cubes
    1 cup heavy cream
    2 teaspoons lemon juice

Melt butter in saucepan and blend in flour, salt and paprika. Gradually stir in water. Add bouillon cubes and cook, stirring, until thickened. Add cream and heat. Remove from heat and stir in lemon juice.

Ginger-Cream Chicken

    4 whole chicken breasts, split
      Flour
      Salt and pepper
      Ground ginger
      Butter *or* margarine
  ¼ cup flour
 1½ cups chicken broth
  ½ cup heavy cream
  2 to 4 tablespoons chopped candied ginger

Shake chicken pieces in bag with flour seasoned with salt, pepper and ground ginger. Brown slowly on both sides in ½ cup butter in large skillet. Cover and cook until tender. Remove to a warm dish and put in slow oven (300°). Add enough more butter to skillet to make ¼ cup. Blend in flour. Gradually add broth and cream and cook, stirring, until thickened. Season to taste with salt, pepper and ground ginger. Pour around chicken and sprinkle with candied ginger. Makes 6 to 8 servings.

Almond Chicken Appetizers

    3 pounds chicken breasts
    1 egg, slightly beaten
    ½ cup milk
    ½ cup all-purpose flour
    ½ teaspoon salt
    ½ teaspoon monosodium glutamate
    Fat for deep frying
    ¼ cup crushed toasted blanched almonds

Remove bones, cut chicken in small pieces and score slightly. Mix
next 5 ingredients until smooth. Dip chicken pieces in the batter.
Drop into hot deep fat (375° on frying thermometer) and fry
until golden brown. Drain and sprinkle with almonds. Serve hot.
Makes about 3 dozen.

Chicken with Almonds and Raisins

    ½ cup blanched whole almonds
    Butter
    ⅓ cup olive oil
    2 large onions, sliced thin
    1 teaspoon salt
    ½ teaspoon pepper
    ¼ teaspoon powdered saffron
    ⅛ teaspoon cayenne
    2 chicken breasts, split
    ½ cup muscat (or other) raisins
    2 teaspoons lemon juice

In skillet, sauté almonds in 1 tablespoon butter until browned;
set aside. Heat oil and ¼ cup butter in heavy heatproof casserole
or Dutch oven. Stir in next 5 ingredients. Add chicken and turn
to coat with onion mixture. Cover and simmer, turning chicken

occasionally, 1½ hours, or until very tender. Remove chicken to shallow serving platter and keep warm. Cook onion mixture, stirring, in casserole over high heat until reduced to a thick sauce. Stir in raisins, lemon juice and almonds and heat through. Pour over chicken. Makes 4 servings.

Stuffed Chicken Breasts

    2 chicken breasts, split, boned and skinned
    1 teaspoon salt
    ¼ teaspoon pepper
    1 teaspoon dried tarragon *or* 3 teaspoons fresh
    ¼ cup butter
    1 egg
      Flour
      Fine bread crumbs
      Sauce (see below)

Flatten the chicken between sheets of waxed paper and sprinkle with salt and pepper on both sides. Combine the tarragon with 2 tablespoons of butter. Chill. Divide into 4 long pieces and place a piece on each chicken breast, turn in edges and roll up. Fasten with toothpicks, if necessary. Mix the egg with a little water. Dip the rolls in the flour, then in the egg, then in the crumbs. Sauté gently in remaining butter for about 20 minutes, turning to brown evenly. Meanwhile make the sauce. Pour some sauce over the chicken. Makes 4 servings.

Sauce

    1 tablespoon flour
    2 tablespoons butter
    ½ teaspoon dried tarragon *or* 1½ teaspoons fresh
    1 teaspoon salt
    1 cup chicken broth
    1 tablespoon lemon juice

Stir the flour into melted butter. Add the tarragon and the salt, and pour in the broth combined with lemon juice slowly while stirring. Taste for seasoning.

Chicken Velvet

        2 chicken breasts
        5 egg whites
        1 teaspoon cornstarch
        ½ teaspoon salt
        ¼ cup water
        3 tablespoons vegetable oil

Remove chicken meat from skin and bones. Cut in 1″ cubes and put in blender with 1 egg white, the cornstarch and salt. Blend until mushy. Gradually add the water, continuing to blend. Beat remaining egg whites until stiff, then gradually fold into chicken mixture. Heat heavy skillet and add oil. Quickly stir 2 tablespoons of the warmed oil into chicken mixture and pour into skillet. Cook over low heat until set but not browned. Makes 4 servings.

Parmesan Chicken Medallions

        3 whole chicken breasts
          Salt and pepper
          Flour
        4 slices firm-textured white bread
        ½ cup freshly grated Parmesan cheese
        2 eggs, beaten
        ¼ to ½ cup clarified butter
          Lemon wedges

Split, bone and skin chicken breasts; place each piece between sheets of waxed paper and pound thin with rolling pin or sides of cleaver. Cut each piece in half crosswise, making 12 chicken scallops, or medallions. Season with salt and a few grindings of pepper. Dust lightly with flour. Remove crusts from bread. Crumble 2 slices at a time into blender and whiz to make fine soft crumbs. Mix with cheese. Dip floured scallops in the egg, then in the crumb mixture. Press to coat chicken evenly, then let dry ½ hour. Heat ¼ cup clarified butter in heavy skillet or sauté pan. Cook scallops over moderate heat until golden on both sides, adding more butter as needed. Serve hot with lemon wedges. Makes 6 servings.

11 *Legs*

Drumsticks used to be for children, either in the nursery or at parties. This is no longer the case. With or without their adjacent thighs, they are first-class food, preferred by those who choose dark meat because it is so moist, flavorful and succulent.

Lemon-Mustard Chicken Legs

    3 tablespoons butter *or* margarine
    4 *each* chicken drumsticks and thighs
    3 tablespoons lemon juice
    3 tablespoons prepared mustard
    ½ cup fine dry bread crumbs
    ½ teaspoon salt
    1 tablespoon grated lemon rind

Melt butter in foil-lined shallow baking pan in 400° oven. Brush chicken with lemon juice, spread with mustard and coat with mixture of last 3 ingredients. Put chicken, skin side down, in the butter and bake 30 minutes. Turn and bake 30 minutes longer, or until well browned. Makes 4 servings.

Chicken Legs Paprika

    4 chicken hindquarters
    1 tablespoon vegetable oil
    1 cup chopped onion
      Salt
    2 teaspoons paprika
    1 chicken bouillon cube
    1 cup boiling water
    1 cup evaporated milk

Using a sharp knife or kitchen shears, separate chicken drumsticks from rest of hindquarters, cutting at joint. Brown chicken in the oil in heavy kettle. Stir in onion and simmer until limp. Season with 1 teaspoon salt and the paprika. Dissolve bouillon cube in boiling water and add to chicken. Bring to boil, cover and simmer 45 minutes, or until chicken is very tender. Stir in evaporated milk and simmer gently just until heated through. Taste and add more salt if necessary. Makes 4 servings.

Sesame Chicken Legs

    4 *each* chicken drumsticks and thighs
    3 tablespoons butter *or* margarine, melted
    ⅓ cup flour
    ½ teaspoon salt
    1 egg beaten with 2 tablespoons water
    ⅔ cup sesame seed

Brush chicken with the butter. Coat with combined flour and salt and dip in egg-water mixture. Roll in sesame seed and put on lightly oiled foil-lined baking pan. Bake at 400° 1 hour and 15 minutes, or until browned. Makes 4 servings.

Oven-Browned Chicken

½ pound onions, sliced thin
16 chicken pieces (drumsticks and thighs)
¼ cup flour
2 teaspoons salt
¼ teaspoon pepper
1 teaspoon paprika
½ cup margarine, melted

Arrange half the onion slices in shallow baking pans. Arrange chicken pieces on onions and top with remaining onions. (Do not pile chicken.) Mix remaining ingredients, except margarine, and sift onto chicken. Pour margarine over top. Bake at 375° 1 hour, or until chicken is browned and tender. Serve with the onions and pan juices. Makes 12 servings.

Chicken Legs in Orange Rice

2½ pounds chicken drumsticks and thighs
3 tablespoons flour
Salt
¼ teaspoon pepper
¼ cup butter *or* margarine
1 cup raw rice
1½ cups water
Grated peel of 1 orange
1 cup orange juice
Chopped parsley

Coat chicken with flour seasoned with 1 teaspoon salt and the pepper; brown slowly in butter in large skillet. Push chicken to one side of skillet. Stir rice into pan drippings, then stir in water, orange peel, juice and ½ teaspoon salt. Bring to boil, cover, then simmer until rice and chicken are tender and liquid is absorbed, about 25 minutes. Sprinkle with parsley. Makes 4 servings.

Rice with Chicken Legs

       6 *each* chicken legs and thighs
         Salt
       3 tablespoons olive oil
      ½ cup chopped onion
       1 clove garlic, minced
       1 green pepper, chopped
       1 can (29 ounces) tomatoes
      ⅓ cup sherry
      ¼ teaspoon pepper
         Pinch of saffron
      ½ teaspoon paprika
       2 whole cloves
       1 bay leaf
    1¼ cups raw rice
       1 package (10 ounces) frozen peas, thawed
       2 tablespoons pimiento strips

Bone legs and thighs. Season each piece with salt and brown in the hot oil in Dutch oven. Add next 3 ingredients and sauté 5 minutes. Add next 7 ingredients and 1 cup water, cover, bring to boil and simmer 15 minutes. Add rice, bring to boil and stir. Cover and simmer 20 minutes. Stir in peas and simmer 5 minutes. Garnish with pimiento. Makes 6 servings.

Drumsticks in Rice Ring

  5 tablespoons margarine
  8 chicken drumsticks
  ⅓ cup buttermilk
  ½ cup cracker meal
   Salt
  ¼ teaspoon pepper
 1½ cups raw rice
  3 cups water
  ½ cup chopped parsley
  1 tablespoon chopped pimiento
  1 envelope chicken gravy mix *or* 1 can chicken gravy

In baking dish, melt 4 tablespoons margarine in hot oven (425°).
Dip drumsticks in buttermilk and shake in bag with cracker meal,
1 teaspoon salt and the pepper. Arrange in baking dish and bake
25 minutes on each side. In large saucepan, bring rice, water,
remaining margarine and 1½ teaspoons salt to boil. Stir once,
cover and simmer 15 minutes, or until liquid is absorbed and
rice is tender. Generously oil a 5-cup ring mold and sprinkle with
parsley and pimiento. Spoon cooked rice into mold and press
down tight with back of spoon. Keep hot by placing mold over
pot of simmering water and placing cover of pot over mold. To
serve, invert mold on heated platter and arrange drumsticks in
center. Serve with gravy mix, prepared as directed on label, or
with heated canned gravy. Makes 4 servings.

Creamy Chicken Thighs with Noodles

    ½ cup chopped dried beef
   12 chicken thighs, skinned
    6 slices bacon, cooked and drained
    1 package (3 ounces) cream cheese, softened
    2 cans (10½ ounces *each*) cream of mushroom
       soup
  1½ cups sour cream
      Chopped parsley
      Hot cooked buttered noodles

Sprinkle dried beef into 3-quart casserole. Arrange chicken thighs, rounded side up, in casserole. Top each with ½ slice bacon. Combine next 3 ingredients and beat until blended. Pour over chicken. Cover tightly with lid or foil and bake in preheated oven at 325° 2 hours. Remove lid and bake uncovered 20 minutes. Sprinkle with parsley and serve on noodles. Makes 6 servings.

Chicken Casserole with Peas

    3 tablespoons butter *or* margarine
  1½ teaspoons paprika
    ¼ teaspoon salt
    ½ teaspoon crushed rosemary
    2 teaspoons soy sauce
    8 chicken thighs
    1 can (4 ounces) sliced mushrooms, drained and
      liquid reserved
      Water
    1 package (10 ounces) frozen green peas
      Hot cooked rice

Preheat oven to 350°. Melt butter in 2-quart casserole in oven. Add next 4 ingredients and mix with butter. Roll chicken thighs in butter mixture and arrange, skin side up, in casserole. Sprinkle with mushrooms. Add enough water to mushroom liquid to measure ½ cup. Pour over chicken, cover and bake 50 minutes. Uncover, add peas and bake 10 minutes. Serve with rice. Makes 4 servings.

Chicken Thigh and Stuffing Bake

    8 chicken thighs
    ¼ cup butter *or* margarine
    ½ cup chopped onion
    ⅓ cup chopped celery
    3 tablespoons chopped parsley
    ¾ teaspoon tarragon
    ½ teaspoon salt
    ⅛ teaspoon pepper
    1 package (7 ounces) cubed stuffing mix
    1 cup water

Brown chicken in butter in large skillet; remove and set aside. Cook onion and celery in drippings until tender. Stir in remaining ingredients and turn into greased 10" x 6" x 2" casserole. Top with chicken, cover with foil and bake at 400° 45 minutes. Uncover; bake 15 minutes longer. Makes 4 servings.

Stuffed Boned Drumsticks

    8 chicken drumsticks
    ¼ pound (4 slices) cooked ham
    1 egg, beaten
    2 tablespoons milk
    ¼ cup white cornmeal
    ¼ cup flour
    ½ teaspoon salt
    ¼ teaspoon pepper
    ¼ cup fat
    1 can (10½ ounces) cream of chicken soup
    2 tablespoons dried parsley

Bone the drumsticks. Cut ham slices in half, making 8 pieces. Roll ham tight and place one roll in center of each drumstick. Roll chicken meat around ham and secure with toothpicks. Dip in mixture of egg and milk and put in bag of cornmeal mixed with flour, salt and pepper. Shake well to coat pieces and brown in melted fat in heavy skillet. Then arrange in greased casserole and top with soup mixed with parsley. Cover and bake at 350° 45 minutes, or until done. Remove toothpicks before serving. Makes 4 servings.

12 *Wings*

A few years ago almost the cheapest parts of the chicken were its wings. They are still reasonable although they are considered gourmet fare over many parts of the world. In America, however, they are often relegated to the soup pot. This is a pity, as you will agree if you try some of these wing dishes.

Parmesan Wings

    4 pounds (about 32) chicken wings
    ½ cup butter *or* margarine
    1 cup flour
    2½ teaspoons salt
    ½ cup grated Parmesan cheese
    ½ teaspoon paprika
    ½ teaspoon oregano
    ⅔ cup buttermilk

Tuck tips of wings under main section. Melt butter in 1 large or 2 medium-size foil-lined baking pans in oven heated to 425°. Mix next 5 ingredients. Dip wings in buttermilk, roll in flour mixture,

then in melted butter. Bake 1 hour, or until very brown and crisp.
Makes 6 to 8 servings.

Chicken Wings in Batter

    2 pounds (about 16) chicken wings
    2 tablespoons butter
    1 teaspoon salt
    1 teaspoon curry powder
    1 cup chicken broth
      Batter (see below)
      Fat for deep frying

Put wings in casserole or baking dish; dot with butter; season
with salt and curry and pour in broth. Bake, covered, in preheated oven at 350°, about 40 minutes. Prepare Batter. Heat
deep fat to 365°. Dip chicken into batter; fry 3 or 4 pieces at
a time in hot fat for 5 minutes, until brown. Drain on paper toweling. Makes 4 servings.

Batter

    1 egg, beaten
    ⅔ cup milk
    1⅓ cups sifted all-purpose flour
    ½ teaspoon salt
    1½ teaspoons baking powder

Beat egg; pour drippings from chicken into measuring cup and
add milk to make ⅔ cup. Add to egg. Sift flour, salt, and baking
powder into egg and milk and beat until smooth.

Broiled Chicken Wings with Barbecue Sauce

  3 pounds (about 24) chicken wings
  2 tablespoons prepared mustard
  ¼ cup cider vinegar
  ¾ cup catsup
  ½ cup molasses
  2 tablespoons vegetable oil
  2 teaspoons Worcestershire sauce
  ½ teaspoon salt
  ¼ teaspoon garlic powder
  ¼ teaspoon hot pepper sauce

Preheat broiler and arrange chicken wings on broiler pan. Combine remaining ingredients to make sauce. Spoon or brush sauce on wings. Broil about 6″ from heat 30 to 40 minutes, turning frequently and keeping tips down, if possible, to prevent burning. Baste frequently with sauce until all is used. Makes 6 servings.

Barbecued Chicken Wings

  2 pounds (about 16) chicken wings
  ⅔ cup Barbecue Sauce (see above)
  2 tablespoons butter *or* margarine, melted
  1½ cups crushed cornflakes
    Salt

Tuck wing tips under larger section. Combine Barbecue Sauce and butter and brush wings with mixture. Roll in cornflake crumbs and sprinkle generously with salt. Put on lightly oiled foil-lined shallow pan and bake at 400° 1 hour and 15 minutes, or until well browned and crisp. Makes 4 servings.

Chicken-Wing Bake with Sweet Potatoes and Pineapple

    4 pounds chicken wings
    ½ cup evaporated milk
    ¾ cup flour
    1 teaspoon salt
    ¼ teaspoon pepper
    ¼ cup margarine
    1 can (1½ pounds) yams, drained
    1 can (15½ ounces) pineapple chunks, drained
      (reserve syrup)
    1 teaspoon soy sauce
    3 tablespoons brown sugar

Dip chicken wings in milk and shake in plastic or paper bag with flour seasoned with salt and pepper. In hot oven (425°) melt margarine in roasting pan. Arrange wings in pan and brown about 25 minutes on each side. Arrange yams and pineapple chunks between wings. Combine reserved pineapple syrup with last 2 ingredients and spoon over all. Bake 25 minutes. Makes 6 to 8 servings.

Chicken Wings and Dumplings

    3 pounds chicken wings
    1 tablespoon vegetable oil
    ½ cup *each* chopped onion, carrot, and celery
      Salt and pepper
    3 chicken bouillon cubes
      Water
    2 tablespoons flour
      Dumpling Batter (see below)

In large heavy kettle, brown wings in the oil. Stir in vegetables and cook, stirring, 10 minutes, or until vegetables begin to brown. Add 1 teaspoon salt and ¼ teaspoon pepper. Dissolve bouillon cubes in 3 cups boiling water. Add to wings and simmer 1 hour, or until meat begins to fall from bones. Taste to correct seasoning. Blend flour with 2 tablespoons water and stir into mixture. Drop dumpling batter by spoonfuls into kettle, forming 8 dumplings. Cover and cook 10 minutes, or until dumplings are done. Makes 6 servings.

Dumpling Batter

    1½ cups biscuit mix
    ½ cup plus 2 tablespoons water
    2 tablespoons chopped parsley

Blend all ingredients together.

Oriental Chicken Wings

    2 pounds chicken wings
    2 scallions, coarsely chopped
    1 tablespoon soy sauce
    ½ teaspoon salt
    1 tablespoon minced ginger
    2 tablespoons peanut *or* vegetable oil
    ½ cup chicken broth
    1 tablespoon minced onion
    1 clove garlic, minced
    1 cup sliced bamboo shoots
    Hot cooked rice

Marinate the chicken wings in a mixture of the remaining ingredients, except the rice, for an hour. Remove the wings to broiler pan and broil 15 minutes. Brush with the marinade, turn, brush again, and broil 15 minutes. Serve on rice with remaining marinade heated and poured over. If you wish to fry the wings, omit oil from the marinade and fry the wings in oil in an iron skillet or wok until brown, add the bamboo shoots and heat and stir. Serve with the rice and sauce as above. Makes 4 servings.

Chinese-Fried Chicken Wings

3 pounds (about 24) chicken wings
2 eggs, slightly beaten
⅔ cup milk
1 cup sifted all-purpose flour
2 tablespoons soy sauce
Vegetable oil for frying
Salt

Using kitchen shears, cut off wing tips, cutting at the joint. Reserve tips for use in soup pot if you wish. Cut the other two sections at joint. At center of each section, cut to the bone all the way around, then make 5 cuts lengthwise from circle to ends. Mix next 4 ingredients until smooth and blended. Dip chicken in batter and fry in hot deep oil (350° on frying thermometer) until browned and crisp. Drain and sprinkle with salt. Makes 4 to 6 servings.

Chicken Wings Indian Style

3 pounds chicken wings
3 tablespoons butter *or* margarine
1 large onion, chopped fine
1 large clove garlic, crushed
1 to 2 tablespoons curry powder
1½ teaspoons salt
½ teaspoon pepper
½ cup grated coconut
2 cooking apples, peeled, cored and diced
1 banana, sliced thin
2 cups chicken broth
2 tablespoons chutney
2 eggs
1 tablespoon water
Hot cooked rice

Brown the wings in butter, turning to brown evenly. Remove and keep warm. Sauté the onion and garlic gently in the drippings for a few minutes, until the onion is soft but not brown. Add 1 tablespoon curry, 1 teaspoon salt, and the pepper. Return wings to the skillet. Add the coconut, apple, banana, and broth. Cover and simmer half an hour. Add chutney and more curry and salt to taste. Stir in the eggs, beaten with the water. Shut off the heat and stir; the egg should be in streaks. Serve with rice. Makes 6 servings.

Chili and Potato-Chip Chicken Wings

    2 pounds (about 16) chicken wings
    3 tablespoons butter *or* margarine, melted
    ½ cup flour
    1 egg, beaten
    2 tablespoons milk
    1½ teaspoons chili powder
    1⅓ cups crushed potato chips

Tuck wing tips under larger section and brush wings with melted butter. Coat with flour and brush with combined egg and milk. Combine chili powder and potato chips and coat wings with mixture. Put on lightly oiled foil-lined shallow pan and bake at 400° 1 hour and 15 minutes, or until well browned and crisp. Makes 4 servings.

13 *Livers*

Years ago, chicken livers cost more than twice as much as calves' liver. Now it is quite the reverse, with chicken livers being about a third as expensive. Of course they are still as much of a luxury (though an inexpensive one) as they ever were—tasty, nutritious, quick cooking and adaptable. In addition, they occupy little space in a freezer, where they keep very well. They are indispensable as hors d'oeuvres, in pâtés and other canapés, and lend glamour to such dishes as omelets; chicken livers in wine make an excellent main course for luncheons, dinners and suppers.

Chicken-Liver Appetizers

- ½ cup soy sauce
- ½ cup water
- ¼ cup sherry *or* sake
- 1 tablespoon sugar
- 1 green onion
- 1 pound chicken livers
- 2 slices fresh ginger
- ¼ teaspoon peppercorns

Mix soy sauce, water, sherry, and sugar and bring to a boil. Cut green onion into ½″ slices and add with chicken livers, ginger and peppercorns. Simmer for 15 minutes. Cool in liquid. Cut livers into pieces and serve on toothpicks as an appetizer. Makes 6 to 8 servings.

Chopped Chicken Livers

½ pound chicken livers
1 cup chicken broth
½ cup minced onion
2 tablespoons butter *or* margarine
2 eggs, hard-cooked, chopped fine
1 tablespoon mayonnaise
Salt
Freshly ground pepper
Lettuce cups (optional)

Cover livers with the broth, bring to boil and simmer 10 minutes, or until done. Drain, cool and chop very fine. Cook onion in the butter, stirring, until lightly browned. Mix liver, onion and eggs well to make a paste. Stir in mayonnaise and season to taste with salt and pepper. Serve in lettuce cups, if you wish. Serves 4 to 6 as appetizer.

Chicken-Liver Pâté with Cognac

½ pound butter
1 pound chicken livers
¼ cup cognac
2 shallots *or* green onions, chopped
½ teaspoon salt
¼ teaspoon pepper
Dash of nutmeg
Hot toast

Melt butter in skillet. Add chicken livers and sauté 8 to 10 minutes, or until done. Put in blender with next 5 ingredients and whirl until well blended. Put in crock or covered dish and refrigerate at least a day and a half before serving with toast. Makes about 2 cups.

Special Chicken Liver Pâté

    1 medium onion, minced
    ½ cup butter
    ½ clove garlic, crushed (optional)
    ½ pound chicken livers
    ½ pound liver sausage (Braunschweiger)
    2 tablespoons water
    2 to 3 tablespoons sherry
    1 teaspoon salt
    ¼ teaspoon pepper
    ⅛ teaspoon oregano
      Crackers, thin dark bread *or* melba toast

Sauté the onion in 2 tablespoons butter until transparent. Add the garlic, if you wish. Add remaining butter and sauté the chicken livers gently with the onion, cooking about 5 minutes. Slice the liver sausage, add and cook 3 minutes. The livers should be soft, not brown. Mash the livers and sausage together in a bowl, using a fork. Add water and 2 tablespoons sherry to the skillet. Stir and scrape to get any brown bits. Return livers to the skillet, stir and blend well. Add seasonings, and more sherry and salt to taste. Put into a serving dish or crock and serve with crackers, thin dark bread or melba toast.

Baked Liver Pâté

    2 eggs, beaten
    2 teaspoons salt
    ½ teaspoon pepper
    1 teaspoon sugar
    ¼ teaspoon *each* ginger, allspice and oregano
    1 pound chicken livers, cut up
    1 medium onion, chopped
    ¼ pound chicken fat *or* butter
    Minced parsley
    Crackers, thin dark bread *or* melba toast

Combine eggs and seasonings and beat until smooth. Mix the livers and onion and sauté gently in the fat or butter for 3 minutes. Whirl in the blender. Pour into a bowl and add the first mixture a little at a time while beating. When thoroughly blended, pour into a 9″ x 5″ x 3″ buttered loaf pan and cover with foil. Set in a larger pan filled with enough hot water to come halfway up the sides of the loaf pan. Bake at 325° for 45 minutes. Remove foil and bake 30 minutes longer. Cool. Run a thin knife or spatula around the edges and turn out on a platter. Garnish with minced parsley. Serve with crackers, thin dark bread or melba toast.

Chicken-Liver Spread

    ½ pound chicken livers
    Water
    ½ teaspoon salt
    1 medium onion, minced
    ½ cup tomato juice
    1 hard-cooked egg, chopped fine
    2 tablespoons chopped parsley
    2 teaspoons lemon juice
    Pepper to taste
    Crackers, thin dark bread *or* melba toast

Cover chicken livers with cold water and add salt. Bring to boil and simmer 4 to 5 minutes. Drain and chop fine. Simmer onion in the tomato juice 15 minutes. Mix all ingredients, except crackers; pack into 1½-cup mold and chill. Unmold and serve with crackers, thin dark bread or melba toast.

Mushroom, Liver and Liverwurst Pâté

> ½ pound chicken livers
> 2 tablespoons butter
> ½ pound mushrooms, sliced thin
> 2 tablespoons chopped green onions *or* chives
> ½ pound liverwurst, sliced
> 2 tablespoons soy sauce
> 2 tablespoons sherry
> 2 teaspoons prepared mustard
> ½ cup sour cream *or* softened cream cheese
> Salt and pepper
> Toast, melba toast, crackers *or* thin dark bread

Sauté the livers slowly in butter for 5 minutes; they should not be browned. Add the mushrooms and green onions and sauté 3 minutes. Add the liverwurst and cook until softened. Whirl briefly in a blender with remaining ingredients, except toast, adding salt and pepper to taste. Serve with toast, melba toast, crackers or thin dark bread.

Sautéed Chicken Livers and Bacon

> 1½ pounds chicken livers, cut in half
> ½ cup flour
> 1 teaspoon salt
> ½ teaspoon pepper
> 6 to 12 slices bacon
> 1 clove garlic, crushed

Dredge the livers or shake, a few at a time, in a paper bag, with a mixture of the next 3 ingredients. Fry the bacon until crisp, remove and set aside. Sauté the livers and garlic in the bacon drippings for 5 minutes, turning to brown livers evenly. Serve topped with the bacon. Good on toast or rice. Makes 6 servings.

Chicken Livers with Bacon in Wine

> 6 slices bacon
> 3 tablespoons minced onion
> ½ green pepper, chopped
> 1½ pounds chicken livers
> ¼ cup flour
> 1 teaspoon salt
> ¼ teaspoon pepper
> ½ cup red wine

Cut the bacon into pieces and sauté until crisp. Remove bacon, drain and keep warm. Sauté the onion and pepper gently in bacon drippings until onions are transparent but not brown. Toss the livers in a mixture of flour, salt and pepper and brown in the same skillet for about 3 minutes. Add the wine, cover and cook 3 minutes. Add the crisp bacon. Makes 6 servings.

Chicken Livers in Champagne

> 1 pound chicken livers
> 3 tablespoons flour
> 1 teaspoon salt
> 1 medium onion, chopped
> 3 tablespoons butter
> 3 scallions, minced
> 1 clove garlic, minced
> ¼ cup water
> 1 cup champagne

Shake the livers in a bag with flour and salt; reserve excess flour mixture. Sauté the onion in butter until transparent. Add scallions, garlic and the chicken livers and sauté gently for 5 minutes. Stir in 2 teaspoons of the leftover flour and the water. Add champagne and heat for 1 or 2 minutes. Makes 4 servings.

Chicken Livers with Brandy

          3 tablespoons flour
          1 teaspoon salt
        ¼ teaspoon pepper
          1 teaspoon monosodium glutamate
          1 pound chicken livers, halved
          6 tablespoons butter *or* margarine
          2 tablespoons brandy

Mix first 4 ingredients. Dredge chicken livers with the mixture and brown quickly in the butter in electric skillet or chafing dish. Reduce heat and cook gently until done and red color has disappeared (livers should be tender, not hard). Just before serving, pour brandy over livers. Makes 4 servings.

Chicken Livers and Mushrooms with Sherry

        1½ pounds chicken livers
          2 teaspoons Worcestershire sauce
        ½ teaspoon Dijon-style mustard
        ½ cup sherry
          1 clove garlic, minced
          3 tablespoons butter *or* bacon fat
        ¼ cup flour
          1 teaspoon salt
        ¼ teaspoon pepper
        ½ teaspoon marjoram *or* oregano
        ½ pound mushrooms, sliced

Cut the livers into about 3 or 4 pieces each and cover with a mixture of Worcestershire sauce, mustard and sherry. Let stand 2 hours, turning several times. Sauté the garlic in butter. Mix the flour, salt, pepper and herb and coat the livers. Sauté in the butter and garlic for 3 minutes, add mushrooms, sauté for 2 minutes while stirring. Add the marinade and any leftover seasoned flour. Heat for a few minutes. Makes 6 servings.

Chicken Livers and Mushrooms

>   2 slices bacon, diced
>   1 medium onion, minced
>   1 pound mushrooms, sliced
> 1½ pounds chicken livers, cut in half
>   3 tablespoons flour
>   1 teaspoon salt
>   1 tablespoon lemon juice
> 1½ cups chicken broth

Sauté the bacon, remove bits and set aside. Sauté onions in the drippings, add mushrooms and livers and sauté for 5 minutes, turning frequently. Blend in the flour and salt; stir in the lemon juice and broth. Cook while stirring until smooth and thickened, about 5 minutes. Add the bacon. Makes 6 servings.

Chicken Livers and Mushrooms on Toast

    ¾ pound chicken livers, halved
    2 tablespoons flour
    ¾ teaspoon salt
    ¼ teaspoon basil
    ⅛ teaspoon pepper
    2 tablespoons minced green onion
    2 cups sliced mushrooms
    3 tablespoons butter or margarine
    ¼ cup heavy cream or half-and-half
    8 slices bread, toasted
      Chopped parsley

Drain livers on paper toweling, then coat with mixture of flour, salt, basil and pepper; set aside. Sauté onion and mushrooms in 1 tablespoon butter in skillet over medium heat until tender, about 4 minutes, stirring occasionally; remove mushrooms and onion and reserve. Melt remaining 2 tablespoons butter in skillet, add livers and sauté until of desired doneness, about 5 minutes. Return mushrooms and onion to skillet, stir in cream and heat. Spoon mushroom-liver mixture on toast and sprinkle with parsley. Makes 4 servings.

Braised Chicken Livers with Rice

    1 pound chicken livers
      Flour
    2 tablespoons butter or margarine
    1 cup chicken broth
      Salt, pepper and rosemary to taste
      Hot cooked brown or white rice
      Chopped parsley

Roll chicken livers in flour and pierce with fork to prevent spattering. Brown lightly in the butter in skillet. Add broth and seasonings and simmer, covered, about 10 minutes. Serve on rice with a sprinkling of parsley. Makes 4 servings.

Chicken Livers and Barley

    1 medium onion, minced
    ½ cup butter *or* margarine
    ½ pound mushrooms, sliced
    1 cup quick-cooking medium barley
    2 cups chicken broth
      Salt and pepper
    1 pound chicken livers

Brown onion lightly in ¼ cup butter in heavy saucepan. Add mushrooms and sauté 5 minutes. Add barley and brown lightly. Stir in broth and bring to boil. Add salt and pepper to taste, cover and simmer 25 minutes, or until barley is tender and liquid absorbed. Sauté chicken livers in remaining butter and season to taste. Stir into barley. Makes 4 to 6 servings.

Creamed Chicken Livers

    ¼ cup flour
    1½ teaspoons seasoned salt
    ½ teaspoon pepper
    1 pound chicken livers
    ¼ cup butter *or* margarine
    ¼ teaspoon paprika
    1½ cups milk, heated

Mix first 3 ingredients. Dip each liver in mixture until well coated. Heat butter until lightly browned, then sprinkle with paprika. Add chicken livers and sauté, turning once, 3 to 4 minutes, or until well browned. Add milk and bring to boil, stirring until thickened. Simmer 2 to 3 minutes. Good on toast. Makes 4 servings.

Chicken-Liver Stroganoff

    4 slices bacon
    1 cup sliced onion
    3 tablespoons flour
    1 teaspoon paprika
    ½ teaspoon salt
    1 pound chicken livers
    1 can (4 ounces) sliced mushrooms, undrained
    ½ cup sour cream
    ¼ cup water
       Hot cooked noodles

Cook bacon until crisp; drain, crumble and set aside. Add onion to drippings and sauté until limp but not browned. Remove onion. Mix 2 tablespoons flour and the seasonings and dredge livers with the mixture. Brown lightly in bacon drippings. Sprinkle livers with any remaining seasoned flour mixture and add bacon, onion and mushrooms. Cover and simmer about 10 minutes. Remove livers to serving platter. Blend remaining tablespoon of flour, the sour cream and the water and stir into pan drippings. Cook, stirring, until thickened. Pour over livers and serve on noodles. Makes 4 servings.

Chicken Livers in Sour Cream

    1 medium onion, sliced
    2 teaspoons gravy seasoning-browning sauce
    ¼ cup butter *or* margarine
    1 pound chicken livers
      Salt and pepper
      Pinch of crumbled rosemary
    1 can (8 ounces) peas
    1 teaspoon cornstarch
    1 cup sour cream

Sauté onion with gravy sauce in the butter in skillet 5 minutes. Add chicken livers, season with salt, pepper, and rosemary, and brown livers. Blend liquid from peas with the cornstarch and stir into mixture. Cook, stirring, until thickened. Add peas and sour cream and heat gently. Makes 4 servings.

Chicken Livers and Noodles with Sour Cream

    2 tablespoons butter
    1 pound chicken livers, halved
    4 scallions, chopped
    1 clove garlic, minced
    ¼ pound mushrooms, thinly sliced
    1 teaspoon salt
    ¼ teaspoon *each* pepper, basil and oregano
    1 cup chicken broth
    1 cup sour cream
      Hot cooked noodles

Melt the butter in a heavy skillet and sauté the livers for 5 minutes, turning to brown evenly. Add the scallions and garlic and cook 3 minutes. Add the mushrooms, season with salt, pepper, basil and oregano, and sauté 3 minutes. Add the broth and simmer 5 minutes. Stir in the sour cream and heat but do not boil. Serve over noodles. Makes 4 servings.

Chicken Livers with Noodles and Cranberries

    1 can (8 ounces) cranberry jelly
    1 can (8 ounces) tomato sauce
    ½ teaspoon garlic powder or small clove garlic, crushed
    1 teaspoon salt
    ¼ teaspoon pepper
    ½ teaspoon oregano or thyme
    1 pound chicken livers, halved
    2 tablespoons butter
    1 package (8 ounces) noodles, cooked

Melt the jelly, add the tomato sauce and seasonings. Sauté the livers in butter, add to the sauce and mix well. Put the noodles on a warm platter and pour livers and sauce over. Makes 4 servings.

Chicken Livers in Chicken Sauce

    1½ pounds chicken livers
    2 tablespoons margarine
    2 small onions, minced
    ½ cup finely diced celery
    1 can (10½ ounces) cream of chicken soup
    ⅓ cup milk
       Chopped parsley
       Toast or rice

Cook chicken livers in the margarine until browned and done. Add onion and celery and cook 2 to 3 minutes. Add soup and milk and heat. Sprinkle with parsley and serve on toast or rice. Makes 4 to 6 servings.

Curried Chicken Livers

        1 pound chicken livers
        1 teaspoon salt
        ½ teaspoon pepper
        ¼ cup flour
        ¼ cup butter *or* bacon fat
        ½ medium onion, minced
        1 tablespoon curry powder
        ½ teaspoon dry mustard
        1 cup chicken broth
           Hot steamed rice

Cut the livers in half. Combine half the salt and pepper with 2 tablespoons flour and roll the livers in the mixture. Sauté in 2 tablespoons butter or bacon fat for 7 minutes, turning several times. Meanwhile sauté the onion in remaining butter until soft; add the curry, mustard, and remaining flour. Pour in the broth slowly, while stirring. Add livers to the sauce and reheat. Reseason to taste with remaining salt and pepper—the amount will depend upon the seasoning in the broth. Serve with rice. Makes 4 servings.

Chicken-Liver Casserole

        4 medium potatoes, cooked, peeled and sliced
           (about 3 cups)
        1 package (10 ounces) frozen cut broccoli, cooked
           and drained
        2 tablespoons butter *or* margarine
        1½ pounds chicken livers, halved
           Salt and pepper to taste
        1 teaspoon marjoram, crushed
        1 cup sour cream
        ½ cup milk

Put potato slices in greased 2-quart casserole and arrange broccoli on top. Heat butter in skillet, add chicken livers and sauté until well browned and done. Sprinkle with the seasonings. Place on top of the broccoli. Add sour cream and milk to skillet and heat gently, stirring to blend in pan drippings. Pour over chicken livers and bake in preheated 425° oven 10 minutes, or until heated through. Makes 6 servings.

Egg and Chicken-Liver Casserole

    1 pound chicken livers
    1 package (2⅜ ounces) seasoned coating mix
        for chicken
    8 hard-cooked eggs, sliced
    1 tablespoon chopped parsley
    1 can (10½ ounces) cream of mushroom soup
    3 tablespoons milk
    6 bacon slices, browned and crumbled

Coat livers with the mix and brown in shallow pan in oven at 400° 15 minutes, or until of desired doneness. Lower temperature to 350°. Arrange eggs in shallow 1-quart baking dish. Top with browned chicken livers and cover with next 3 ingredients, mixed together. Bake 20 minutes, or until heated through, and sprinkle with bacon bits. Makes 6 servings.

Chicken-Liver Mixed Grill

    6 slices bacon
    2 large baking potatoes, cut crosswise into ½" slices
        Salt, pepper and marjoram
 1½ pounds chicken livers
    8 mushroom caps
   12 cherry tomatoes
        Drained capers (optional)

Preheat broiler unit. Line broiling pan with foil. Arrange bacon in pan and broil, not too close to unit, turning once, about 5 minutes. Remove bacon to plate. Arrange potato slices in bacon fat and season lightly with salt, pepper and marjoram. Broil about 10 minutes, then turn potato slices, season and push to side of pan. Add chicken livers, season and broil 10 minutes. Add mushrooms and cherry tomatoes and broil 5 minutes. Reheat bacon last 2 minutes of broiling. If desired, sprinkle each serving with capers. Makes 4 to 6 servings.

Sweet and Pungent Chicken Livers

    1½ pounds chicken livers
    3 tablespoons vegetable oil
      Salt and pepper
    3 green peppers, diced
    2 cups chicken broth
    1 can (13¼ ounces) pineapple chunks *or* tidbits,
      drained
    3 tablespoons cornstarch
    3 tablespoons cider vinegar
    2 tablespoons sugar
    1 to 2 tablespoons soy sauce
      Hot cooked rice

Wipe chicken livers with absorbent paper, then sauté in hot oil in skillet 6 minutes, or until well browned. Season with salt and pepper. Add next 3 ingredients and bring to boil. Blend cornstarch with vinegar and add with sugar to hot mixture. Cook, stirring, until thickened and clear. Add soy sauce to taste. Serve with rice. Makes 6 servings.

Chicken Livers with Fruit

>   1 can (17 ounces) fruit cocktail
>   1 can (3 ounces) chopped mushrooms
>   2 slices bacon
>   2 tablespoons margarine
>   2 tablespoons minced onion
>   2 packages (8 ounces *each*) frozen chicken livers,
>   thawed, *or* 1 pound fresh
>   2 tablespoons flour
>   1 teaspoon lemon juice
>   1 teaspoon chopped parsley
>   Hot cooked rice

Drain fruit cocktail and mushrooms, reserving liquids. Cook bacon and drain on absorbent paper; crumble. Add margarine to bacon drippings in skillet. Add mushrooms and onion and cook slowly 5 minutes. Add chicken livers and bacon. Cook 10 minutes, turning livers once. Remove livers and mushrooms to a hot serving dish and keep warm. Stir flour into drippings in skillet. Add reserved liquids and lemon juice, fruit cocktail and parsley. Cook, stirring, until smooth. Serve with rice. Makes 6 servings.

Chicken Livers with Vegetables

>   1 pound chicken livers, halved
>   2 tablespoons flour
>   Salt
>   Pepper
>   2 green onions with tops, minced
>   2 tablespoons butter
>   ½ pound mushrooms, sliced
>   1 cup cherry tomatoes
>   1 can (17 ounces) small green peas, drained
>   Thyme (optional)

Blot livers on absorbent paper, then coat with flour seasoned with ½ teaspoon salt and ⅛ teaspoon pepper. Sauté livers and onion in butter in large skillet until livers are lightly browned, about 5 minutes. Add mushrooms and sauté until golden, about 4 minutes, stirring occasionally. Add tomatoes and heat just until they start to burst, about 2 minutes. Add peas and heat 2 minutes. Reseason to taste, adding thyme if desired. Makes 4 servings.

Sautéed Chicken Livers with Peas and Carrots

¼ cup flour
1 teaspoon salt
¼ teaspoon pepper
½ teaspoon poultry seasoning
1 pound chicken livers, halved
¼ cup butter *or* margarine
¾ cup chicken broth *or* bouillon
1 box (10 ounces) frozen peas and carrots, cooked

Mix first 4 ingredients and dredge livers with the mixture. Heat butter in skillet, add livers and sauté until browned. Add broth and simmer a few minutes. Add vegetables, cover and heat. Makes 4 servings.

Chicken-Liver Omelet

1 green onion, sliced
6 small mushrooms, sliced, *or* 1 can (3 ounces) sliced mushrooms, drained
2 tablespoons butter
½ pound chicken livers, cut up
2 teaspoons flour
2 tablespoons dry white wine
Salt and pepper
6-egg omelet

Sauté onion and mushrooms in the butter. Push to side of skillet and add livers. Cook, stirring, until just cooked through. Mix with mushrooms and onion and sprinkle with flour. Stir in wine and heat gently, stirring, until slightly thickened. Season with salt and pepper, fill omelet and put remainder around sides. Makes 4 servings.

PART III

Foreign
Recipes

14 *With a Foreign Accent*

Chicken is very popular in foreign lands. While in some countries another meat may be *numero uno*—veal in Germany and Italy, pork in the Orient, lamb in the Near East and beef in England—chicken usually comes next. And, perhaps because it is Number Two, people try harder when creating their regional specialties.

Nowadays one needn't travel around the world in order to enjoy exotic dishes, for the ingredients in the following recipes are available in our modern markets. Nor need one worry about the expense, because most of these recipes originated among people who are far from being millionaires.

In France, or here at home, there's the popular *Coq au Vin*, while Germany prefers her favorite brew in *Huhn in Bier*. One doesn't have to be Italian or a hunter to prepare *Chicken Cacciatore*, nor Belgian to enjoy *Waterzooie*. Both Austria and Hungary claim *Chicken Paprikash* while *Paella* and *Arroz con Pollo* mean Spain or Latin America. Without bothering to cross the Pacific one can try Japan's *Sukiyaki* or China's *Mandarin Chicken*. One can even transform plain dishes by dressing them in foreign sauces, from the conventional *à la king* to Indian curry.

Coq au Vin Blanc
(Chicken in White Wine)

    2 chickens, about 3 pounds *each*, cut up
    1 teaspoon salt
    ¼ teaspoon pepper
    2 tablespoons butter
    2 medium onions, sliced very thin
    ½ pound mushrooms (optional)
    2 tablespoons flour
    ¼ cup chicken broth
    ¾ cup dry white wine
      Parsley

Sprinkle the chicken with salt and pepper and sauté in butter for about 20 minutes. Add onions and cook 5 minutes; then add mushrooms, if you wish, and cook 3 minutes longer. Blend the flour with broth and stir in, add the wine, cover and simmer about 20 minutes, until the chicken is tender. Garnish with parsley. Makes 6 servings.

Coq au Vin Rouge
(Chicken in Red Wine)

    ½ pound diced salt pork
      Water
    ¼ cup butter
    2 fryers, about 3 pounds *each*, cut up
    1 teaspoon salt
    ¼ teaspoon pepper
    ½ pound small mushrooms
    1 pound white boiling onions
    4 shallots, minced
    2 cloves garlic, minced
    3 tablespoons flour
   2½ cups red wine
      Minced parsley

Boil the pork for 3 or 4 minutes in a small amount of water. Remove pork and sauté in butter in an ovenproof heavy pot. When brown, remove the pork bits and set aside. Bone the chicken if you wish, and sprinkle with salt and pepper and brown in the butter. Remove and keep warm. Add mushrooms and onions to the pot, cover and simmer for 20 minutes. Add shallots and garlic and stir in the flour. Pour in the wine slowly while stirring. When smooth and slightly thickened, add the chicken and diced pork and bake at 350° for an hour. Reseason and garnish with parsley. Makes 8 servings.

*Short-Cut Coq au Vin Rouge

> 1 large onion, sliced
> 2 tablespoons butter
> 3 slices bacon
> ¼ cup flour
> 1 can (10½ ounces) chicken broth
> ½ cup red wine
> 3 cups diced cooked chicken
> Hot cooked rice

Sauté the onion gently in butter until transparent but not brown. Fry the bacon, remove and set aside. Add bacon drippings to onion and stir in the flour. When blended, pour in the broth while stirring. When smooth and thickened, add the wine and chicken and heat. Top with crumbled bacon. Serve with rice. Makes 6 servings.

*Blanquette of Chicken

    3 tablespoons butter
    4 tablespoons flour
    1½ cups chicken broth
    ½ cup half-and-half
    ½ teaspoon salt
    ½ teaspoon celery salt
    3 cups diced cooked chicken
    2 egg yolks
    3 tablespoons cream
    1 tablespoon minced parsley

Melt the butter, blend in the flour, and pour in the broth and half-and-half slowly while stirring. Add salt and celery salt. Stir and cook until smooth and thickened. Add the chicken and heat several minutes. Beat the egg yolks with the cream. Add a little of the chicken sauce, stir, and return all to the pot. Add the parsley and cook gently for 2 minutes. Do not boil. Makes 6 servings.

*Chicken Poulette

    2 cups sliced *or* diced cooked chicken
    ½ pound mushrooms, sliced thin
    2 tablespoons flour
    3 tablespoons butter
    ½ teaspoon salt
    1 cup chicken broth
    1 egg yolk
    ⅓ cup heavy cream
      Juice of ½ lemon

Put the chicken in a baking dish and add the mushrooms. Blend the flour into melted butter. Add salt and pour the broth in slowly while stirring. Simmer until the sauce is thickened and smooth, pour it over the chicken and bake at 350° for 20 minutes. Mix the egg yolk with the cream, stir it in and bake 10 minutes. Add the lemon juice just before serving. Makes 4 servings.

Poulet en Cocotte

    2 broiler-fryers, 2½ to 3 pounds *each*, cut up
    ¼ cup prepared mustard
    1 tablespoon horseradish
    1 teaspoon fines herbes (parsley, tarragon, chervil, etc.)
      Salt to taste
    ¼ cup butter
    ¾ cup water
    ¾ cup dry white wine
    4 teaspoons flour

Rub chicken pieces with mixture of mustard and horseradish, herb seasonings and salt. Melt butter in heavy pot or Dutch oven. Add chicken and brown in oven at 500° 15 minutes on each side. Reduce heat to 350°, add water and wine and bake 30 minutes longer, or until done. Remove chicken and thicken juices with flour-and-water paste, to make a thick gravy. Pour over chicken. Makes 4 to 6 servings.

Chicken Breasts en Coquilles

        2 whole chicken breasts
          Salt
        2 sprigs parsley
        1 slice *each* lemon and onion
        ½ cup chicken broth
        ½ cup dry white wine
        ½ pound scallops
        2 tablespoons finely chopped green onion
        3 tablespoons butter *or* margarine
        2 tablespoons flour
          Salt, pepper and nutmeg
        ½ cup heavy cream
        ¼ cup shredded Gruyère cheese
        2 to 4 tablespoons grated Parmesan cheese

Season chicken with salt and wrap in foil with parsley, lemon and onion slices and broth. Steam-poach in preheated 350° oven 50 to 60 minutes, or until done. Reserve liquid, cool chicken and peel off skin. Remove bones and pull meat into thin strips. Bring wine to simmer, add scallops and poach 2 to 3 minutes. Remove scallops and reserve liquid. Sauté green onion in the butter 2 to 3 minutes. Blend in flour, then stir in strained broth from cooking chicken and liquid from scallops. Cook, stirring, over low heat until slightly thickened. Season lightly with salt, pepper and nutmeg. Put back over heat and stir in cream and Gruyère. Add about ½ cup sauce to the chicken in individual ramekins or a shallow broiler-proof baking dish. Quarter scallops and arrange on top. Pour remaining sauce over mixture and sprinkle with Parmesan cheese. Put low under broiler until bubbly hot and flecked with brown. Makes 6 servings.

Chicken Breasts en Gelée

>   4 whole chicken breasts, halved
>   Salt
>   1½ cups chicken broth
>   1 carrot, peeled and sliced
>   1 slice onion
>   2 whole cloves
>   1 sprig parsley
>   ½ teaspoon tarragon
>   1 envelope unflavored gelatin
>   ¼ cup Madeira
>   Lemon juice
>   1 cup black grapes
>   Long thin strips of lemon peel
>   Orange peel
>   Chicory or other salad greens

Sprinkle chicken very lightly with salt and put, skin side up, in skillet or saucepan. Add next 6 ingredients. Bring to boil, cover and simmer 30 minutes, or until tender. Cool slightly in broth and pull off skin. (Lift meat off bones, if desired.) Wrap chicken in foil or plastic and chill. Chill broth enough to skim off fat layer and strain. There should be 1½ cups. If necessary, add water to make up amount. Sprinkle gelatin on broth in skillet. Stir over low heat 2 to 3 minutes, or until melted. Add Madeira, a few drops lemon juice, and salt, if needed. Chill until syrupy. Brush lightly on chicken breasts. Halve and seed a few black grapes. Press, cut side down, on chicken in a pretty flower design, using lemon peel for stems. Put a small piece of orange peel in center of each grape flower. Glaze with film of thick (but not set) aspic. It requires about ½ cup aspic. If desired, chill remaining aspic in shallow pan until firm. Cut in tiny cubes and pile around chicken on platter. Garnish with remaining grapes and chicory. Makes 4 to 6 servings.

Chicken Breasts Cordon Bleu

    3 whole chicken breasts, split, boned and skinned
      Salt and pepper
    4 tablespoons (1 small can) pâté de foie gras *or*
      liver pâté
    6 slices prosciutto
      Flour
    2 eggs, beaten
    1 cup fine dry bread crumbs
    4 to 6 tablespoons butter
    2 tablespoons cognac
    ½ cup dry white wine

Place breasts between sheets of waxed paper and pound thin
with heavy knife or side of cleaver. Season each with salt and
pepper and spread center with pâté. Lay each split breast on
same-size prosciutto slice, press down firmly, then roll up. Dust
lightly with flour and dip in eggs. Roll in bread crumbs to coat
evenly, then set aside to dry ½ hour. Cook gently in butter in skillet 6 to 8 minutes, or until golden on all sides. Remove and keep
warm. Pour cognac into skillet and ignite it. Add wine and stir
and simmer a minute or two. Pour over chicken. Makes 6 servings.

Normandy Chicken

    2 broiler-fryers, about 3½ pounds *each,* cut up or
      quartered
    2 teaspoons salt
    ¼ teaspoon pepper
    ½ cup butter
    1 cup dry apple cider
    ¼ cup flour
    1 cup half-and-half
    ½ cup heavy cream
      Sautéed apple slices

Sprinkle the chicken with salt and pepper and brown in 3 table-spoons butter, turning to brown evenly. Add the cider, cover and simmer half an hour. When the chicken is tender, remove it and keep warm. Add remaining butter to the pan and blend in the flour. Pour in the half-and-half slowly while stirring. Add the cream, heat, and pour over the chicken. Garnish with apple slices. Makes 8 servings.

Paella

   1 pound chicken breasts
   1 pound chicken thighs
   1 pound chicken legs
  ½ cup olive oil
   2 large onions, chopped
   2 cloves garlic, minced
   2 cups raw rice
   3 cups chicken broth
  ½ teaspoon saffron
   2 teaspoons salt
  ½ teaspoon pepper
  ½ pound Spanish sausage, sliced
   2 dozen cherrystone clams
   2 dozen raw shrimp, shelled
   3 large tomatoes, peeled and quartered
   1 package (10 ounces) frozen peas
  ½ small can pimientos, cut into strips

Brown all the chicken pieces in oil, turning to brown evenly. Remove and keep warm. Sauté the onion and garlic until onion is transparent but not brown. Add the rice and stir and cook until it is pale brown. Add the broth, saffron, salt and pepper. Cover and simmer 10 minutes. Rub a large flat casserole or paella pan with a little oil. Put in half of the sausage, clams, shrimp, tomatoes, and rice mixture. Place the chicken pieces on top with remaining sausage, clams, shrimp, tomatoes, and half the peas.

Arrange remaining rice with remaining peas around the chicken with pimientos. Bake at 350°, covered, for 15 minutes. If you don't have a cover to fit, use foil. Uncover and bake 15 minutes more; this can be done over low heat on top of the stove. Add a little more broth if needed. Makes 8 servings.

Easy Paella

    3 chicken breasts, boned and quartered
    ¼ cup oil
    ¼ teaspoon saffron
      Water
    2 teaspoons salt
    ¼ teaspoon pepper
    2 medium onions, chopped
    1 green pepper, chopped
    2 cloves garlic, minced
    1 can (10 ounces) whole clams *or* 1 pound soft clams
    2 cups instant rice
    ¾ pound cleaned shrimp
    2 tablespoons minced parsley

Brown the chicken lightly in oil. Dissolve the saffron in 2 tablespoons boiling water and let stand. Season the chicken with salt and pepper. Add onions, green pepper and garlic to the chicken. Sauté until onions are light brown and the chicken almost done. Add the juice from the canned clams (if used) and 2 cups water. If using fresh clams, scrub and add. Heat; stir in the rice. Cover and cook 5 minutes, until rice is done. Add the shrimp and clams and cook, covered, for 3 minutes. Sprinkle with parsley. Makes 6 servings.

Arroz con Pollo I
(Rice with Chicken)

        1 teaspoon oregano
        2 peppercorns
        1 clove garlic, peeled
     3¼ teaspoons salt
        2 teaspoons olive oil
        1 teaspoon vinegar
        1 broiler-fryer, 2½ to 3 pounds, cut up
        2 ounces ham, diced fine
        1 ounce salt pork *or* 1 slice bacon, diced fine
        1 tablespoon lard *or* other fat
        1 medium onion, chopped
        1 green pepper, chopped
        1 chili pepper, seeded and chopped
        2 leaves cilantro (fresh coriander) *or* parsley, chopped
        6 green olives, pitted and chopped
        1 teaspoon capers
        1 tomato, peeled and chopped
       ¼ cup tomato sauce
     2¼ cups raw rice
        1 can (17 ounces) peas
          Water
        1 can (4 ounces) pimientos

Mash oregano, peppercorns, garlic, salt, olive oil and vinegar together in mortar and rub into chicken pieces. Brown ham and
salt pork in hot lard in Dutch oven or large kettle. Add chicken
and brown lightly. Add onion, peppers, cilantro, olives, capers
and tomato. Cook over low heat 10 minutes, stirring occasionally.
Add tomato sauce and rice and cook 5 minutes. Drain liquid from
peas, measure and add enough water to make 3 cups. Reserve
peas and heat liquid to boiling. Add liquid to Dutch oven, mix
well and cook rapidly, uncovered, for 2 minutes. With large spoon
turn rice from bottom to top. Cover and cook slowly 20 minutes.
Add peas, again turn rice, cover and cook 10 minutes. Heat pimientos, drain and garnish rice. Makes 6 servings.

Arroz con Pollo II

> 1 chicken, 4½ to 5 pounds, cut up
> 3 tablespoons vegetable shortening
> 1 onion, minced
> 1 teaspoon salt
> ½ teaspoon sugar
> 3 medium tomatoes, peeled and chopped, *or*
>   1 (10 ounce) can tomatoes
> 3 sweet potatoes, cut into 3″ pieces
> 3 potatoes, peeled and cut into 2″ pieces
> 2 cups rice
> 3 cups chicken broth *or* water *or* combination

Sauté the chicken in shortening, turning to brown on all sides. Add the onion and sauté 5 minutes, until pale brown. Add salt, sugar and tomatoes and simmer 5 minutes; add sweet potatoes, potatoes and rice. Mix well and add the broth and/or water. Cover tightly and simmer 30 minutes. Serve on a warm platter, raking the rice onto the platter with a fork to keep it fluffy. Makes 6 to 8 servings.

Spanish Chicken and Rice with Sausage

> 2 chorizos (Spanish sausages)
>   Water
> 2 tablespoons vegetable oil
> 1 frying chicken, 3 pounds, cut up
> 1 medium onion, chopped
> 1 cup raw rice
> 2 cups hot chicken broth
> 1 cup cooked chick-peas
> 1 box (10 ounces) frozen green peas
>   Salt and coarsely ground black pepper
>   Black-olive halves (optional)

Put sausages in Dutch oven with small amount of water. Cover and simmer until water is evaporated, then brown sausages on all sides. Remove from Dutch oven, slice and set aside. Put oil in same pan and heat. Add chicken and brown very well. Remove and set aside. Scrape bottom of Dutch oven to loosen any brown bits. Add onion and rice and cook, stirring, until both are lightly browned. Add chicken and sausage and pour broth over top. Cover and bake in moderate oven at 350° 30 minutes, or until chicken is tender. Add chick-peas, green peas, and salt and pepper to taste. Mix lightly with fork. Cover and put back in oven. Turn off heat and leave in oven about 20 minutes. Sprinkle with olives, if desired, and serve from Dutch oven. Makes 4 servings.

Pollo Mexicano
(Mexican Chicken)

> 3 chicken breasts, split
> 2 cups water
> 2 teaspoons salt
> 1 large onion, chopped fine
> 1 green pepper, chopped fine
> 1 clove garlic, minced
> 1 tablespoon butter
> 1 can (1 pound) tomatoes, drained
> 2 cans (4 ounces *each*) button mushrooms, drained
> 1 teaspoon chili powder
> 1 teaspoon oregano
> ½ teaspoon pepper
> 1 teaspoon sugar
> 1 tablespoon cornstarch

Put the chicken in a pot with water and salt. Simmer, covered, for 40 minutes or until tender. Remove chicken and, when cool enough to handle, remove skin and bones. Put the skin and bones back into the pot and simmer uncovered for 15 minutes to strengthen and reduce the broth. Strain. Sauté the onion, pepper and garlic in butter until the onion is soft but not brown. Add the tomatoes and remaining ingredients except the cornstarch. Add the broth and simmer uncovered for 15 minutes. Mix cornstarch with a little cold water and stir in. Cook and stir for 2 minutes. Adjust seasoning. Put the chicken in and serve as soon as heated through, or put the chicken in a baking and serving dish, pour the sauce over and heat in the oven at 400° until bubbling. Makes 6 servings.

Pollo con Chorizos
(Mexican Chicken with Sausage)

> 2 broiler-fryers, 2½ to 3 pounds *each,* cut up
> 3 chorizos *or* sweet Italian sausages, sliced
> ½ cup dry white wine
> 3 cups chicken broth
> 3 tablespoons margarine
> 1 cup dry bread crumbs

Put the chicken and sausage in a Dutch oven or casserole with all of the remaining ingredients. Cover and simmer for 45 minutes or until the chicken is tender. Makes 6 servings.

Chicken Casserole, Mexican Style

> 2 whole chicken breasts, split
> Seasoned salt
> Seasoned pepper
> 2 cans (10½ ounces *each*) cream of chicken
>   soup
> ½ teaspoon oregano
> ¼ teaspoon *each* ground cumin, sage, chili powder
>   and garlic powder
> Vegetable oil
> 1 package (1 dozen) corn tortillas
> 1 can (4 ounces) green chilies, diced
> 1 pound longhorn (Cheddar) cheese, shredded
> 2 large onions, coarsely diced

Sprinkle chicken with seasoned salt and pepper and wrap in foil, sealing edges securely. Set in baking pan and bake at 350° 1 hour, or until chicken falls from bones. Cool, reserving liquid, and dice chicken. Mix liquid with soup and the seasonings; heat and set aside. Heat a small amount of oil in skillet. Dip each tortilla in the oil until softened, then drain on absorbent paper. Grease bottom of 2½-quart casserole and overlap 3 tortillas evenly in bottom of dish. Add one-fourth each of chicken, chilies, cheese, onions and soup mixture. Repeat layers of tortillas and other ingredients until all are used. Bake at 375° 35 minutes, or until mixture bubbles around edges. Makes 6 servings.

Chili Chicken

>   2 frying chickens, 2½ to 3 pounds *each*, quartered
>   3 tablespoons vegetable oil
>   1 large onion, chopped
>   1 clove garlic, minced
>   1 can (16 ounces) tomato sauce
>   2 cups water
>   1 tablespoon chili powder
>   1 can (17 ounces) chick-peas, drained

Brown chicken quarters in oil. Remove chicken, add onion and garlic to pan and brown. Add tomato sauce, water and chili powder. Bring to boil, return chicken to pot, cover and simmer 45 minutes. Add chick-peas and simmer 15 minutes. Makes 8 servings.

*Mexican Tamale Pie

>   1 cup yellow cornmeal
>   1 cup milk
>   3 cups water
>   Salt
>   2 slices bacon, diced
>   ½ cup *each* chopped celery, onion and green pepper
>   1 can (1 pound) tomatoes *or* 2 cups diced peeled
>   fresh tomatoes
>   ½ cup leftover corn (optional)
>   ¼ cup sliced pimiento-stuffed green *or* pitted
>   black olives
>   2 to 3 teaspoons chili powder
>   2 cups chopped leftover cooked poultry
>   Pepper to taste
>   1 cup shredded Cheddar cheese

Mix cornmeal and milk and stir into the boiling salted water. Cook, stirring, until thickened, then cover and simmer 10 minutes. Spoon into shallow 2-quart baking dish, mounding around edges; set aside. Sauté bacon until crisp. Add celery, onion and green pepper and sauté until tender. Add salt to taste and remaining ingredients, except cheese, and simmer, covered, 5 minutes. Spoon into center of baking dish. Sprinkle with cheese and bake in preheated 350° oven 30 minutes, or until brown and bubbling. Makes 4 to 6 servings.

Portuguese Chicken

        3 pounds chicken breasts and thighs
    1½ teaspoons salt
    ½ teaspoon pepper
        3 tablespoons vegetable oil
        3 onions, chopped
        1 green pepper, chopped
        1 cup raw rice
        2 tablespoons chopped coriander *or* flat-leaf parsley
        2 cups chicken broth
    ½ pound pork sausage meat

Sprinkle the chicken with salt and pepper and brown in oil in a casserole or skillet with a cover, turning to brown evenly. Remove and keep warm. Sauté the onions and pepper in the same oil until onions are transparent but not brown. Stir in the rice, coriander or parsley, and the broth. Meanwhile, brown the sausage, crumbling it with a fork. Add sausage and chicken to the skillet. Stir, cover and bake at 375° for half an hour. Uncover and bake 10 minutes. Makes 6 servings.

Portuguese Fricassee

> 1 chicken, 3 pounds, cut up
> Flour
> Salt and pepper
> 3 tablespoons olive oil
> 1 large onion, chopped
> 1 large clove garlic, minced
> ½ teaspoon cumin
> 1 cup chicken broth
> ¼ cup white wine, vermouth *or* dry port
> 15 stuffed olives, sliced or halved

Dust the chicken with flour mixed with salt and pepper (reserve excess) and brown in olive oil. Remove chicken to a heavy pot or a casserole. Sauté the onion in the oil until transparent but not brown. Add the garlic, cumin and broth, and stir and scrape bits from the bottom of the skillet. Pour over the chicken in the casserole. Simmer covered for half an hour, then add wine mixed with a little of the seasoned flour. Add the olives and simmer 10 minutes, uncovered. Reseason to taste. Good with rice. Makes 4 servings.

Galinha À Portuguès
(Braised Chicken in Cream)

> 4 onions, chopped fine
> 3 tablespoons butter
> 2 tablespoons olive oil
> 1 teaspoon salt
> ¼ teaspoon pepper
> 1 teaspoon fresh minced tarragon *or* ½ teaspoon dried
> ¾ cup dry port wine
> 6 chicken breasts *or* 8 to 10 thighs
> ½ cup chicken broth
> 1 cup cream

Sauté the onion in mixture of 2 tablespoons butter and 1 table-spoon oil until soft. Add salt and pepper, the tarragon and ½ cup of port. Simmer 5 minutes. Meanwhile, sauté the chicken in re-maining butter and oil for 20 minutes, turning frequently. Add the chicken broth and the onion-port sauce. Cover and simmer 10 minutes. Add the cream and the remaining port, reheat, and reseason to taste. Makes 6 servings.

Portuguese Chicken with Sausage

¾ pound Portuguese (linguica) *or* Polish sausage
2 tablespoons vegetable *or* olive oil
2 broiler-fryers, 2½ to 3 pounds *each*, cut up
2 cloves garlic, crushed
1 large onion, minced
2 cups shredded cabbage
1½ teaspoons salt
½ teaspoon pepper
    Pinch red pepper
2 cans (1 pound *each*) plum tomatoes

Sauté the sausage until brown. Remove and set aside. Add oil to the pan and brown the chicken, turning to brown evenly. Transfer chicken to a baking dish or casserole. Add garlic and onion to the drippings and brown lightly; add cabbage and cook 1 minute while stirring. Add the salt, pepper, red pepper and tomatoes and simmer 2 or 3 minutes. Pour over the chicken, cover and bake at 375° for an hour. Makes 6 servings.

Chicken in Port from Portugal I

        2 chicken breasts, boned, skinned and split
        1 teaspoon salt
        ¼ teaspoon pepper
        ¼ teaspoon nutmeg
        ¼ cup flour
        2 tablespoons butter
        2 tablespoons oil
        2 tablespoons water
        1 cup heavy cream
        ½ cup port wine

Flatten the breasts between pieces of waxed paper, using a rolling pin, mallet or bottle. Combine the next 4 ingredients and rub the mixture into the chicken. Sauté in butter and oil for about 15 minutes, turning to brown evenly. Remove chicken and set aside. Add water and then cream to the pan; stir and simmer for 3 or 4 minutes. Add the wine and chicken, cover and simmer about half an hour, until the chicken is tender. (If you want thicker juices, add a little of the leftover flour made into a paste with a little port or water.) Makes 4 servings.

Franco con Porto
(Chicken in Port from Portugal II)

        2 broiler-fryers, 3 pounds *each*, cut up
        3 tablespoons butter
        3 tablespoons flour
        2 cloves garlic, minced
        1 teaspoon salt
        ¼ teaspoon pepper
        1 teaspoon coriander
        2 cups port wine (preferably white)
        1 cup cream

Brown the chicken in butter in a Dutch oven or casserole. Remove and set aside. Brown the flour and garlic in the drippings, adding the salt, pepper and coriander. Stir in the port and add the chicken. Simmer, covered, for 45 minutes. Stir in the cream and reheat. Makes 6 servings.

Huhn in Bier
(German Chicken in Beer)

> 1 broiler-fryer, about 3 pounds, cut up
> ½ cup flour
> 1 teaspoon salt
> ¼ teaspoon pepper
> 1 medium onion, sliced thin
> 3 tablespoons butter
> 1½ cups beer
> ½ cup heavy cream

Roll the chicken in a mixture of flour, salt and pepper. (You may shake in a paper bag instead, if you wish.) Reserve excess. Brown the chicken and onion in butter. Turn the chicken to brown on all sides and stir the onions. Add the beer and simmer, covered, for 45 minutes. Add the cream, reheat and adjust seasoning. Add a little of the reserved seasoned flour if you want a thicker sauce. Makes 4 servings.

Baked Broilers German Style

> 2 broilers, 2½ to 3 pounds *each,* quartered
> 2 teaspoons salt
> 2 eggs
> 1 tablespoon water
> 1 cup bread crumbs
> ½ cup grated Parmesan *or* Swiss cheese
> ¼ cup butter
> ¼ cup vegetable oil
> Juice of 1 or 2 lemons

Sprinkle the chicken with salt. Beat the eggs with the water. Mix the crumbs with the cheese. Dip pieces of chicken in egg and then crumb mixture. Brown in a mixture of butter and oil, turning to brown thoroughly on all sides. Place in a roasting pan to bake at 400° for half an hour. Sprinkle with lemon juice. Makes 4 to 6 servings.

*German Chicken in Patty Shells

> 8 patty shells
> 3 tablespoons flour
> 3 tablespoons butter
> 1 cup chicken broth
> ½ teaspoon salt
> ¼ teaspoon pepper
> 2 egg yolks
> ¼ cup heavy cream
> 2½ cups diced cooked chicken
> ½ pound mushrooms, sliced, *or* 1 can (4 ounces) button mushrooms, drained

Buy the patty shells from a bakery, get frozen ones, or make them. Blend the flour with melted butter, then pour in the broth slowly while stirring. Season with salt and pepper. Beat the yolks with the cream, add to sauce and simmer until smooth. Add the chicken and mushrooms. Reheat and fill patty shells, letting some sauce run over. Makes 8 servings.

CHICKEN PAPRIKASH

The Hungarians make theirs with sour cream, the Austrians with fresh cream, but in either case, Hungarian paprika is indicated as it is much sweeter than the Spanish or other varieties.

Chicken Paprikash

> 3 onions, chopped
> 3 tablespoons butter
> 1 to 3 tablespoons Hungarian paprika
> 1 teaspoon salt
> ½ teaspoon basil
> 2 broiler-fryers, 2½ to 3 pounds *each*, cut up
> 1 cup chicken broth
> 2 tablespoons flour
> 1½ cups sour cream

Sauté the onions in butter until transparent. Stir in the paprika, salt and basil. Add the chicken. Brown and stir for 15 minutes. Pour in the broth, cover and simmer for about 25 minutes, until tender. Stir the flour into the sour cream and stir very slowly into the gravy. Heat without boiling. Add more paprika to taste. Good with noodles or spaetzle. Makes 6 servings.

Paprika Huhn
(German Chicken Paprika)

> 2 medium onions, chopped
> 3 tablespoons butter
> 2 broiler-fryers, 2½ to 3 pounds *each*, cut up
> 1 tablespoon Hungarian paprika
> 1 teaspoon salt
> ¼ teaspoon pepper
> 3 tablespoons flour
> 2 cups chicken broth
> ½ cup heavy cream
> 2 tablespoons chopped fresh dill *or* 2 teaspoons dried
>   dill weed
> ½ cup sour cream

Sauté the onions in butter until softened. Add the chicken, sprinkle with paprika, salt and pepper and sauté until browned,

turning frequently, about 10 minutes. Cover and cook gently for
15 minutes. Combine the flour with broth and half the heavy
cream, pour over, add half the dill and simmer, covered, for 15
minutes, until chicken is tender. Remove to a deep serving dish
and keep warm. Combine remaining cream with the sour cream
and add to the gravy. Stir and heat without boiling for 5 minutes.
Pour over the chicken and sprinkle with remaining dill. Makes
6 servings.

Austrian Paprika Chicken

       1 chicken, about 3½ to 4 pounds, cut up
       1 teaspoon salt
       ¼ teaspoon pepper
       ¼ cup chicken fat *or* butter
       1 large onion, thinly sliced
       2 tablespoons Hungarian paprika
       ¼ pound mushrooms, sliced
       1 cup heavy cream

Sprinkle the chicken with salt and pepper and brown in chicken
fat for 20 minutes, turning frequently to brown evenly. Stir in
the onion and paprika and sauté for 5 minutes. Add the mushrooms and cook 5 minutes longer. Add cream, turn the heat very
low and heat but do not boil. Makes 4 servings.

Viennese Chicken Paprikash

    1 large onion, diced
    3 tablespoons butter *or* margarine
    1 teaspoon salt
    1 tablespoon Hungarian paprika
    ⅛ teaspoon red pepper
    1 broiler-fryer, 3 to 3½ pounds, cut up
    ¼ cup chicken broth
    ¼ cup tomato sauce *or* 2 tablespoons tomato puree
    ¾ cup heavy cream *or* 1 cup yogurt

Sauté the onion in butter until transparent, add salt, paprika and red pepper, and stir. Add the chicken and brown on all sides for about 10 to 15 minutes. Add the broth and tomato sauce, cover and simmer for about half an hour, until the chicken is tender. Remove chicken to a deep hot serving dish and keep warm. Stir in the heavy cream slowly; heat and stir but do not boil. Adjust seasoning to taste and pour over the chicken. Makes 4 servings.

Papriká Scsirke
(Hungarian Chicken Paprika)

    ¼ cup butter
    4 large onions, chopped
    1 to 2 teaspoons Hungarian paprika
    2 broiler-fryers, 3 pounds *each*, cut up
    1 teaspoon salt
    ¼ teaspoon pepper
    Water
    Chicken broth *or* bouillon cube
    2 tablespoons flour
    1 pint sour cream
    Spaetzle *or* noodles

Melt the butter in a heavy kettle. Sauté the onions until transparent; do not brown. Stir the paprika into the onions. Add the chicken, salt and pepper; stir for a few minutes and then add 1 cup water. Cover tightly and cook for half an hour. If there is not enough liquid, add a cup of chicken broth or a cup of water and a chicken bouillon cube and cook until tender, about 20 minutes longer. Stir the flour into the sour cream. Add a little hot gravy to this mixture and then pour it back into the pot with the chicken while stirring. Heat and stir; do not let boil. Taste for seasoning and add paprika and/or salt if desired. Serve with spaetzle or noodles. Makes 6 servings.

Pollo alla Cacciatore I
(Italian Chicken Hunter's Style)

> 2 broiler-fryers, about 3 pounds *each*, cut up
> 1 teaspoon salt
> ¼ teaspoon pepper
> Flour
> 3 tablespoons olive oil
> 2 medium onions, finely chopped
> 1 green pepper, chopped
> 2 cloves garlic, crushed
> 1 bay leaf
> ½ teaspoon sugar
> ¼ cup water
> 1 can (1 pound) Italian tomatoes
> ¾ cup wine, white or red
> ¼ pound mushrooms, sliced

Sprinkle the chicken with salt and pepper and dredge with a little flour. Sauté in oil, turning to brown evenly. Add the onion, green pepper, garlic, bay leaf and sugar and simmer a few minutes. Add the water, tomatoes and wine and simmer, covered, for 30 minutes, until the chicken is tender. Add the mushrooms and cook 10 minutes more. Reseason. Makes 8 servings.

Chicken Cacciatore II

>   1 frying chicken, about 3 pounds, cut up
> ¼ cup olive *or* vegetable oil
>   2 onions, sliced
>   2 cloves garlic, crushed
>   1 can (1 pound) Italian tomatoes
>   1 can (8 ounces) tomato sauce
>   1 teaspoon salt
> ¼ teaspoon pepper
>   1 teaspoon crushed oregano
>   2 bay leaves
>   Italian-style grated cheese

Brown chicken on all sides in the hot oil in large deep skillet.
Remove chicken and keep warm. Cook onion and garlic in oil
remaining in skillet until lightly browned. Add remaining ingredients, except cheese, and simmer 5 minutes. Put chicken back
in skillet and cook, covered, 45 minutes, or until tender. Arrange
chicken on hot platter. Skim excess fat from sauce and remove
bay leaves; pour over chicken. Serve with cheese. Makes 4 servings.

Chicken Cacciatore III

>   1 broiler-fryer, 3 pounds, cut in serving pieces
>   1 teaspoon monosodium glutamate
>   1 teaspoon salt
> ½ teaspoon paprika
> ¼ teaspoon pepper
>   1 medium onion, sliced
>   1 clove garlic, minced
>   1 medium green pepper, cut in strips
>   1 can (1 pound) tomatoes
>   1 can (3 or 4 ounces) chopped mushrooms, undrained
> ¼ teaspoon *each* ground allspice and thyme
>   2 tablespoons chopped parsley

Sprinkle chicken pieces with monosodium glutamate, ½ teaspoon salt, the paprika and pepper. Put under broiler, turning once, 10 minutes, or until browned on both sides. Mix remaining salt with onion, garlic, green pepper, tomatoes, mushrooms with their liquid, allspice and thyme in large skillet; bring to boil, cover and cook 10 minutes. Add chicken, cover, reduce heat and simmer 40 minutes, or until chicken is tender. Sprinkle with parsley. Makes 4 servings.

Breast of Chicken Italian Style

    3 chicken breasts, skinned, boned, and split
      Flour
    ½ teaspoon salt
    6 slices ham
    ¼ cup butter
    ½ cup chicken broth
    ½ cup Marsala *or* sweet vermouth

Flatten the breasts between pieces of waxed paper. Dust with flour and salt. Put a slice of ham on each chicken fillet. Roll up and fasten with toothpicks. Sauté in butter for about 10 minutes, turning to brown evenly. Add broth and wine and simmer, covered, for 10 minutes. Pour drippings over the chicken when serving. Makes 6 servings.

Milanese Breast of Chicken

       3 chicken breasts, skinned, boned, and split
         Lemons
         Salt and pepper
         Flour
       2 eggs, well beaten
       1 cup fine dry bread crumbs
       2 tablespoons salad oil
      ¼ cup butter
         Minced parsley
         Lemon quarters

Place chicken between sheets of waxed paper and pound thin
with rolling pin or side of cleaver. Rub with cut lemon, season
with salt and pepper and dust lightly with flour. Shake off excess,
then dip in eggs. Drop into crumbs and turn to coat evenly. Refrigerate 1 hour. Heat oil and butter in large heavy skillet. Add
chicken—do not crowd—and cook over moderate heat 4 to 6 minutes on each side, or until crispy gold and tender. Watch heat
carefully. Place crisp chicken on hot platter and sprinkle with
parsley. Serve at once with lemon quarters. Makes 6 servings.

Easy Italian-Style Chicken Legs

       4 chicken legs with hindquarters
       1 tablespoon vegetable oil
       1 onion, quartered and sliced
       1 clove garlic, crushed
       1 can (1 pound) tomatoes
      ½ large green pepper, cut in strips
       1 teaspoon basil
      ½ teaspoon oregano
         Salt and pepper to taste

Using a sharp knife or kitchen shears, separate chicken legs from hindquarters, cutting at joint. In large skillet, brown chicken in the oil. Add onion and garlic and cook until lightly browned. Add remaining ingredients and simmer 35 minutes, or until chicken is very tender. Makes 4 servings.

Chicken, Scallopini Style

    2 chicken breasts, boned and split
    3 tablespoons flour, seasoned with salt and pepper
    3 tablespoons olive oil
    ¼ cup sherry
    1 lemon, thinly sliced
    2 teaspoons capers

Pound chicken breasts very thin between 2 sheets of waxed paper. Dredge with seasoned flour and brown 3 minutes on each side in hot olive oil in skillet over medium heat. Pour off excess oil. Add sherry, top with lemon slices and capers and simmer 5 to 6 minutes more, or until tender. Makes 4 servings.

Chicken with Ravioli

    1 broiler-fryer, about 3 pounds, cut up
    2 tablespoons butter *or* oil
      Salt and pepper
    ¼ cup water
    1 medium onion, chopped
    1 medium clove garlic, crushed
    ¼ teaspoon crushed oregano
    ½ cup green-pepper strips
    2 cans (14½ ounces *each*) beef ravioli in meat sauce

Brown chicken on both sides in the butter in skillet. Season lightly with salt and pepper. Add next 4 ingredients. Cover and simmer 30 minutes, or until chicken is tender. Add green pepper and ravioli and simmer, stirring occasionally, 15 minutes longer. Makes 4 to 6 servings.

Chicken-Gizzard Spaghetti

    1 cup chopped onion
    1 clove garlic, crushed
    1 tablespoon bacon fat
  1½ pounds gizzards, chopped
    ⅓ cup chopped parsley
    1 teaspoon basil
    ½ teaspoon oregano
    1 teaspoon salt
  2¾ cups water
    1 package (2¼ ounces) spaghetti-sauce mix
    1 can (6 ounces) tomato paste
    ¼ teaspoon crushed red pepper
    ½ pound thin spaghetti, cooked

In large kettle, simmer onion and garlic in the bacon fat. Add gizzards, herbs, salt and 1 cup water. Bring to boil, cover and simmer 45 minutes, or until gizzards are tender. Combine 1¾ cups water and remaining ingredients, except spaghetti. Stir into gizzards and simmer about 30 minutes. To serve, toss sauce in bowl with cooked spaghetti. Makes 6 servings.

INDIAN COOKING

When one thinks of Indian cuisine, one usually thinks of curry, and why not, since almost every dish contains it? However, the quantity used varies, and the spices that make up curry vary a great deal. This is true not only in different districts in India, but also from house to house. Each housewife and chef mixes his own. Here we buy blended curry powder, but the blends are not all alike in flavor. Try different ones for a variety of tastes.

Moorgee Masalah
(Indian Chicken Curry I)

> 2 whole chicken breasts and 4 legs, cut up
> 2 cloves garlic, crushed
> 1 cup chopped onion
> 1 teaspoon salt
> 3 tablespoons peanut *or* vegetable oil
> 1 cup tomato puree
> 3 tablespoons curry powder
> Water *or* chicken broth (optional)
> 1 teaspoon ground ginger
> 2 teaspoons sesame seeds
> 1 teaspoon cardamom
> 1 teaspoon cinnamon
> 1 tablespoon ground poppy seed
> 1 teaspoon paprika
> Cooked rice

Put the chicken in a large skillet with garlic, onion, salt and 2 tablespoons oil. Sauté for a few minutes. Add the tomato puree and curry. Simmer for about 45 minutes, until the chicken is tender, adding a little water or chicken broth if it gets too dry. Using as many spices and seeds as are available, heat them in the remaining oil in a skillet and add to the chicken for the last 15 minutes of cooking. Adjust seasoning. Serve with rice. Makes 6 servings.

Moorgee Kari
(Indian Chicken Curry II)

    2 broiler-fryers, 2½ to 3 pounds *each*, cut up
    ½ cup flour
    2 teaspoons paprika
    1 tablespoon curry powder
    1 teaspoon salt
    ¼ teaspoon pepper
    ¼ cup oil, margarine *and/or* butter
    2 onions, chopped
    1 clove garlic, minced
    3 cups chicken broth *or* 3 cups water and
       3 chicken bouillon cubes
    1 cup grated coconut
    1 cup raisins
    1 banana, sliced
  1½ cups raw rice
    ¼ cup chopped nuts (optional)

Roll the chicken in a mixture of flour, paprika, 2 teaspoons curry, salt and pepper. Coat well on all sides. Brown in oil, margarine or butter, or a mixture. Remove chicken to a deep kettle or Dutch oven. Brown the onions in remaining drippings for 3 or 4 minutes, add garlic and add to the chicken. Add remaining curry and remaining ingredients, except nuts. Stir well, cover and bake at 350° for an hour. Top with a few chopped nuts if you wish. Makes 6 servings.

Indian Chicken Curry III

>   1 roasting chicken, about 5 pounds
>   1½ quarts water
>   1 cup chopped celery and leaves
>   5 onions, coarsely chopped, divided
>   2 teaspoons salt
>   2 medium apples, peeled and chopped
>   ¼ cup butter
>   ¼ cup flour
>   3 tablespoons curry powder
>   1 cup seedless raisins
>   1 banana, sliced
>   ¾ cup cream
>   2 eggs, beaten
>   Rice
>   Chutney and condiments (see page
>   202 for suggestions)

Simmer the chicken in water with the celery, 1 onion and 2 teaspoons salt for about an hour, until almost tender. When cool
enough to handle, take the chicken off the bones in large pieces
and defat the broth. Sauté the apples and remaining onions in
butter until soft but not brown, blend in the flour, add the curry
and about 4 cups of the reserved defatted broth. Add the raisins
and banana and return chicken to the pot. Heat and stir until
the sauce is thickened and smooth. Add cream and reheat, but
do not boil. Stir in the eggs just before serving. They give a
streaked, opaque look. Serve with rice and chutney and other
condiments of your choice. Makes 6 to 8 servings.

Curried Chicken

> 1 broiler-fryer, about 3 pounds, cut up
> Salt, pepper and flour
> 2 tablespoons butter *or* margarine
> 1 tablespoon minced onion
> 2 teaspoons curry powder
> 1 tablespoon tomato paste
> Juice of 1 lemon
> 3 whole cloves
> Small piece of bay leaf
> 1½ cups chicken broth

Sprinkle chicken lightly with salt and pepper, then roll in flour. Heat butter in skillet, add chicken and brown on both sides. Remove chicken, add onion and sauté a few minutes. Stir in curry powder and tomato paste and heat, stirring, a few seconds. Add remaining ingredients and bring to boil. Add chicken, cover and simmer 40 minutes, or until tender. Add a little water if necessary to make additional gravy. Good with steamed rice. Makes 4 servings.

*Quick Chicken Curry

> 1 can (10½ ounces) cream of chicken soup
> ½ cup half-and-half
> 1 clove garlic, crushed
> 1 tablespoon curry powder
> 2 cups diced cooked chicken
> 2 tablespoons grated coconut
> Hot rice

Mix the soup and half-and-half, garlic and curry, cover and simmer for 10 minutes. Add the chicken and coconut and heat through. Adjust seasoning. Serve with rice. Makes 4 servings.

Coconut-Curry Chicken

> ⅓ cup frozen orange-juice concentrate, thawed
> 1 teaspoon salt
> 1 egg, slightly beaten
> 1 broiler-fryer, 2½ to 3 pounds, cut up
> 1 cup crushed cornflakes
> ½ cup shredded coconut
> 1 teaspoon curry powder
> ¼ cup butter, melted
>   Orange slices

Mix first 3 ingredients, add chicken and marinate 15 minutes. Remove chicken; reserve marinade. Mix next 3 ingredients and coat chicken with mixture, pressing it on. Put on lightly oiled foil-lined pan and drizzle with butter combined with reserved marinade. Cover pan with foil and bake at 350° 30 minutes. Uncover and bake 30 to 40 minutes longer, or until well browned. Serve on platter with garnish of orange slices. Makes 4 servings.

Curried Chicken Breasts

> 3 whole chicken breasts, split and boned
> ½ cup margarine *or* part butter
> 2 medium apples, peeled and cut up
> 1 large onion, chopped
> 2 tablespoons grated coconut
> ½ banana, sliced
> ¾ cup half-and-half
> 1 to 2 tablespoons curry powder
> ½ teaspoon salt
>   Hot cooked rice

Brown the chicken in margarine, turning to brown evenly. Remove. Add the apple and onion to the drippings. Cook until onion is limp but not brown. Add the coconut and banana, then the half-and-half, curry and salt. Return chicken to the pot, cover and simmer about 25 minutes, until tender. Serve with rice. Makes 6 servings.

Curried Chicken and Tomatoes

 ¼ cup flour
 1 teaspoon salt
 ¼ teaspoon pepper
 1 broiler-fryer, about 3 pounds, cut up
 2 tablespoons *each* margarine and vegetable oil
 ½ cup chopped celery
 1 small onion, chopped
  Few sprigs parsley, chopped
 1 clove garlic, minced
 1½ teaspoons curry powder
 ½ teaspoon thyme
 1 can (1 pound) tomatoes
 3 tablespoons raisins
  Hot cooked brown or white rice

Mix first 3 ingredients and coat chicken pieces with the mixture. Brown on all sides in the margarine and oil in skillet. Remove chicken. Add next 6 ingredients and cook, stirring occasionally, until celery is tender. Add tomatoes and bring to boil. Put chicken back in skillet and spoon mixture over top. Cover and simmer 15 minutes. Uncover, add raisins and simmer 15 minutes longer, or until chicken is tender. Serve with the rice. Makes 4 servings.

Curried Honey Chicken

 ¼ cup margarine, melted
 ½ cup honey
 ¼ cup prepared mustard
 1 teaspoon *each* salt and curry powder
 2 frying chickens, about 3 pounds *each*, cut up
  Hot cooked rice

Mix all ingredients, except chicken and rice, and roll chicken in the mixture. Put, skin side up, in roasting pan. Bake at 375°, basting occasionally with drippings in pan, about 1 hour. Serve with rice. Makes 6 to 8 servings.

Indian Curried Pot-Roasted Chicken

>   1 roasting chicken, 4 to 5 pounds
>   Salt and pepper
>   ½ teaspoon ground ginger
>   5 tablespoons butter *or* margarine
>   1 can (10½ ounces) condensed chicken broth
>   1 medium onion, minced
>   1 tart apple, peeled and chopped
>   1 tablespoon curry powder
>   2 tablespoons flour
>   1 cup milk
>   1 tablespoon lemon juice
>   Hot cooked rice

Tie chicken legs together, then bring string around chicken to make compact. Season with salt, pepper and the ginger. In large heavy kettle, brown chicken lightly on all sides in 2 tablespoons butter. Add chicken broth and bring to boil. Cover and simmer about 15 minutes. Cook onion and apple in remaining butter, stirring, about 5 minutes. Blend in curry powder and add to chicken. Cover and simmer, turning once or twice, 45 minutes longer, or until tender. Remove to platter and keep hot while preparing sauce. Mix the flour and milk until smooth and gradually add to sauce in kettle, stirring. Cook a few minutes, or until thickened. Stir in lemon juice and serve with the chicken and rice. Makes 6 servings.

*Leftover-Chicken Curry

>   2 tart green apples, peeled, cored, diced
>   1 large Spanish onion, chopped
>   1 to 3 tablespoons curry powder
>   3 tablespoons butter *or* margarine
>   1 can (10½ ounces) cream of mushroom soup
>   1 cup sour cream
>   2 cups diced cooked chicken
>   Salt
>   Hot cooked rice
>   Condiments (see page 202 for suggestions)

In top part of double boiler over direct heat, cook apples, onion and curry powder in the butter 2 to 3 minutes. Blend in soup and sour cream, then add chicken. Put over boiling water and heat well, stirring occasionally. Add salt to taste and serve with rice and condiments. Makes 4 servings.

Curried Chicken-Spaghetti Casserole

>   3 tablespoons flour
>   2 tablespoons curry powder
>   2½ teaspoons salt
>   ¼ teaspoon pepper
>   1 broiler-fryer, about 3 pounds, cut up
>   ⅓ cup oil
>   1 large onion, sliced
>   1 clove garlic, crushed
>   2½ cups water
>   1 package (8 ounces) spaghetti, broken into thirds
>   Chopped parsley

Mix flour, curry powder, salt and pepper in paper bag; add chicken a few pieces at a time and shake to coat (reserve leftover flour mixture). Heat oil in large skillet over medium-high heat and brown chicken; remove to platter. Sauté onion and garlic in drippings until tender, then stir in reserved flour mixture, the water and spaghetti. Add chicken and bring to boil; reduce heat, cover and simmer 20 minutes, or until chicken and spaghetti are tender. Sprinkle with parsley. Makes 4 to 6 servings.

Traditional Condiments for Curry

> Chutney
> Grated coconut
> Chopped nuts
> Raisins
> Sliced banana
> Sliced apple
> Scallions or onions, chopped fine
> Crumbled crisp bacon
> Fresh ginger, chopped fine
> Grated hard-cooked egg

Choose several condiments, always including chutney if available.

Waterzooie
(Belgian Chicken in a Pot)

> 1 chicken, 4 to 5 pounds
> Juice of 1 lemon
> Water
> 3 leeks *or* 5 scallions, cut up
> 3 stalks celery, cut up
> 2 tablespoons chopped parsley
> 2 teaspoons salt
> ½ teaspoon pepper
> 2 cups dry white wine
> ¼ cup bread crumbs

Rub the chicken with lemon juice and put into a large heavy pot with water to half-cover. Add leeks, celery, parsley, salt and pepper and simmer for about 45 minutes, covered. Add the wine, cover and simmer half an hour until the chicken is very tender. Remove chicken and, when cool enough to handle, remove skin and bones, leaving the meat in large serving pieces. Return to the soup with bread crumbs. Be sure each serving has pieces of chicken in it. Makes 6 servings.

Chicken Strips Madeira

>2 whole chicken breasts, split, boned and skinned
>6 tablespoons butter *or* margarine
>Salt, freshly ground pepper, nutmeg
>1 chicken liver, quartered
>1 cup sliced fresh mushrooms
>1 teaspoon lemon juice
>¼ cup minced onion
>½ cup chicken broth
>2 tablespoons tomato puree
>½ cup Madeira
>2 tablespoons minced parsley

Place breasts between sheets of waxed paper and flatten slightly with rolling pin or side of cleaver. Cut each in strips about ½″ wide. Brown lightly, a few pieces at a time, in 2 tablespoons butter. Remove to warm dish and season with salt, pepper and a dash of nutmeg. Keep warm. Cook liver in same pan until lightly browned; set aside. Heat 2 tablespoons butter in same pan. Add mushrooms, stir until shiny, then sprinkle with lemon juice. Cook gently 2 minutes. Add to chicken strips. Heat remaining butter in same pan; add onion and cook until soft. Blend in chicken liver, broth, tomato puree and Madeira. Cook 5 minutes, or until flavors are well blended. Reseason. Add chicken and mushrooms, heat gently and sprinkle with parsley. Serve at once. Good with steamed brown rice. Makes 4 servings.

Greek Chicken with Onions

        2 tablespoons butter
        2 tablespoons vegetable oil
        2 broiler-fryers, about 2½ pounds *each*, cut up
          Salt and pepper
       18 small onions, peeled
        2″ cinnamon stick
        4 cloves
        ½ cup seedless raisins
        1 cup red wine
        2 tablespoons red wine vinegar
        1 teaspoon ground cumin
        1 clove garlic, pressed
        1 can (6 ounces) tomato paste

Heat butter and oil in a casserole and brown chicken. Season with salt and pepper and remove. In fat, sauté onions, stirring. Replace chicken, add cinnamon and cloves. Sprinkle raisins over all. Combine remaining ingredients, stirring to blend well. Pour sauce over casserole. Bake, covered, in preheated 350° oven for 1 hour, or until chicken is tender. Remove cinnamon stick and cloves. Makes 6 servings.

Middle-Eastern Chicken with Cracked Wheat

        2 broiler-fryers, about 3 pounds *each*, cut up
        2 tablespoons butter
        2 tablespoons vegetable oil
          Salt and pepper
        3 medium onions, chopped
        1 clove garlic, chopped
       1½ cups cracked wheat
        ½ teaspoon ground coriander
          Juice and grated rind of 1 lemon
        3 cups boiling chicken broth

Brown chicken in a casserole in butter and oil. Season with salt and pepper and remove. Cook onion and garlic in fat until translucent. Add cracked wheat, then remaining ingredients except broth, stirring to mix well. Replace chicken, covering it with bulgur (cracked wheat) mixture. Pour broth over contents of casserole. Bake, covered, in preheated 350° oven for 1 hour. Makes 6 to 8 servings.

*Armenian Chicken and Rice Pilaf

⅔ cup raw rice
3 tablespoons butter *and/or* chicken fat
1 cup chicken broth
2 cups drained canned tomatoes
Salt to taste
¼ teaspoon pepper
⅛ teaspoon sugar
1½ to 2 cups diced cooked chicken

Cook the rice in butter or chicken fat or a combination, until the rice is brown. Add the broth slowly while stirring. Cook until the liquid is absorbed, then stir in the tomatoes and seasonings. The amount of salt will depend upon the seasoning in the broth. Start with less than 1 teaspoon and taste. Stir in the chicken and reheat. Makes 4 servings.

*Chicken Pilaf

> 2 cups diced cooked chicken
> ¼ cup butter
> ¼ cup coarsely chopped nuts
> 2 tablespoons minced onion
> 1 teaspoon salt
> ¼ teaspoon pepper
> 2 cups raw rice
> 4 cups chicken broth
> 2 tomatoes, peeled and chopped

Cook chicken in butter over low heat for 3 minutes. Add nuts and cook for 2 minutes longer. Add onion, salt and pepper. Add rice and cook for 5 minutes, stirring. Pour in boiling broth. Add tomatoes, bring to boil, cover and simmer for 20 minutes. Makes 4 servings.

*Chicken–Fried Rice Pilaf

> 1½ cups rice
> ¼ cup butter
> 3 cups chicken broth
> 2 to 2½ cups finely diced cooked chicken
> Salt and pepper

Sauté the rice in butter until light brown. Pour in the broth while stirring. Cover and simmer for 15 minutes. Stir in the chicken; add salt and pepper to taste. Cook 5 minutes, turn off heat and let stand for 5 minutes longer. Makes 6 servings.

Chicken Stroganoff

>   2 broiler-fryers, 2½ to 3 pounds *each*, cut up
>   ½ cup flour
>   1½ teaspoons salt
>   ¼ teaspoon pepper
>   1 teaspoon paprika
>   ½ cup butter
>   ½ pound mushrooms
>   ½ cup chicken broth
>   1½ to 2 cups sour cream

Shake the chicken in a bag with a mixture of the flour, salt, pepper and paprika. Reserve excess flour mixture. Sauté the chicken in 4 tablespoons butter, turning to brown evenly. Cover and cook gently for half an hour. (You may, instead, cover and cook in the oven at 350° for 40 minutes if you wish.) If the mushrooms are large, slice or cut into quarters; if small, leave them whole. Sauté in remaining butter for 4 or 5 minutes. Stir in the remaining seasoned flour. Add the broth slowly while stirring. Add the sour cream, stir, and add the chicken. Heat but do not boil. Makes 6 servings.

Chicken Kiev I

>   3 chicken breasts, skinned, boned, and split
>   Salt
>   ⅓ cup butter
>   2 teaspoons dried tarragon *or* 1 tablespoon fresh
>   2 tablespoons minced chives
>   2 tablespoons minced parsley
>   Pepper
>   Flour
>   1 egg mixed with 1 tablespoon of water
>   Fine bread crumbs
>   Fat *or* oil for deep frying

Flatten the chicken between pieces of waxed paper with a rolling pin, the side of a cleaver or a bottle. Sprinkle with a little salt. Cream the butter with tarragon, chives, parsley, salt and pepper. Chill. Divide into 8 long pieces and place one on each chicken fillet. Roll breasts around the butter, tucking in the sides to make a tightly sealed roll; secure with toothpicks, if necessary. Roll in flour, then egg mixture, then the crumbs. Fry in deep fat or oil until golden, 8 to 10 minutes. Remove with a slotted spoon; never use a fork. Drain on paper toweling. Makes 6 servings.

Chicken Kiev II

        3 chicken breasts, about 1 pound *each*
        ½ cup butter *or* margarine, softened
        2 teaspoons minced green onion
        2 teaspoons minced parsley
        ½ teaspoon salt
        1 clove garlic, minced
        ¼ cup flour
        1 egg beaten with 2 tablespoons water
        ¾ cup fine dry bread crumbs
          Vegetable oil
          Lemon wedges (optional)

Split, skin and bone breasts. Place each breast between layers of heavy-duty foil and flatten gently with mallet, taking care not to tear chicken. Combine butter and next 4 ingredients and form into roll ¾" in diameter. Wrap and chill until firm, then cut in 6 slices and place one in center of each piece of chicken. Roll up tightly, tucking in ends, and secure with toothpick or skewer. Dip each roulade first in flour, then in egg mixture and finally in bread crumbs. Chill thoroughly. In skillet, heat about 1½" vegetable oil. Fry chicken, turning occasionally, until golden. Place in hot oven (400°) about 10 minutes. Remove skewers before serving. Serve with lemon wedges, if desired. Makes 6 servings.

Syrian Chicken with Dates

> 2 tablespoons butter
> 2 tablespoons vegetable oil
> 2 broiler-fryers, about 3 pounds *each*, cut up
>   Salt and pepper
> 1 cup orange juice
>   Juice of 1 lemon
> 2 cups chicken broth
> 3 tablespoons cornstarch
> 1 teaspoon salt
> ½ teaspoon pepper
> 1 teaspoon curry powder
> 1 medium onion, chopped
> 12 to 18 pitted dates, cut in halves lengthwise

Heat butter and oil in a casserole and brown chicken. Season with salt and pepper and remove. Combine remaining ingredients except dates, mix well in the casserole, and cook, stirring, until sauce thickens. Replace chicken. Bake, covered, at 350° for 45 minutes. Arrange dates on top of chicken. Bake, covered, 15 minutes. Makes 6 to 8 servings.

Baked Peanut-Butter Chicken from Malaysia

> 1 broiler-fryer, about 3 pounds, cut up
> ¼ cup flour
> 1 egg
> ⅓ cup smooth *or* crunchy peanut butter
> 1 teaspoon salt
> ⅛ teaspoon pepper
> ⅓ cup milk
> ½ cup fine dry bread crumbs
> ¼ cup vegetable oil

Dip chicken in the flour. Blend next 4 ingredients. Gradually add milk, beating with fork to blend. Dip chicken in peanut-butter mixture, then in crumbs. Put on lightly oiled foil-lined baking pan. Drizzle oil over chicken pieces. Bake at 375° 45 minutes, or until browned and crisp. Makes 4 servings.

Chicken in Peanut-Butter Sauce

    1 broiler-fryer, 3 to 3½ pounds, quartered
    ¼ cup flour
    1 teaspoon salt
    ⅛ teaspoon pepper
    ¼ cup vegetable oil
    1 medium onion, chopped
    1 clove garlic, minced
    1 cup water
    ½ cup peanut butter
    1 can (8 ounces) tomato sauce
    1 tablespoon sugar
    1 tablespoon vinegar
    1 teaspoon chili powder

Wash and dry chicken. Mix flour, salt and pepper. Dredge chicken with the mixture and brown on all sides in hot oil in skillet. Remove chicken and brown onion and garlic lightly in oil remaining in skillet. Blend in remaining ingredients and add chicken pieces. Simmer, covered, 40 minutes, or until chicken is tender. Makes 4 servings.

South Pacific Chicken

    1 cup well-drained canned crushed pineapple
        (reserve syrup)
    1 can (1 pound) red kidney beans, whirled in
        blender or food processor
    ¼ cup sugar
    1 tablespoon honey
    1 teaspoon soy sauce
    1 teaspoon monosodium glutamate
    Vegetable oil
    Salt and pepper
    1 clove garlic, minced
    2 broiler-fryers, about 3 pounds *each*, cut up
    ½ cup flour

Mix first 6 ingredients and ¼ cup vegetable oil. Add 1 teaspoon salt, ¼ teaspoon pepper and the garlic. Dredge chicken with the flour mixed with 1 teaspoon salt and ¼ teaspoon pepper. Brown on all sides in hot oil. Drain and, using tongs, coat each piece with some of pineapple mixture. Put on baking sheet and bake at 350° about 45 minutes. Makes 8 servings.

Chicken and Rice from Central Africa

    3 tablespoons instant minced onion
    ¾ teaspoon instant minced garlic
    Water
    2 frying chickens, about 2½ pounds *each*, cut in
        serving pieces
    2 tablespoons vegetable oil
    1 cup coconut milk (see Note) *or* milk
    2 teaspoons salt
    ¼ teaspoon cayenne *or* red pepper
    5 whole cloves
    ½ teaspoon cinnamon
    1 cup raw rice
    Chopped parsley

Mix first 2 ingredients and 3 tablespoons water. Let stand 10 minutes to rehydrate. Brown chicken well on all sides in the oil in Dutch oven. Add 2 cups water and remaining ingredients, except last 2. Bring to boil, cover and simmer 20 minutes. Add rice, cover and simmer, stirring occasionally, 25 minutes longer, or until rice and chicken are tender. Sprinkle with parsley. Makes 6 servings.

NOTE To make coconut milk, combine 1 can (4 ounces) shredded coconut and 1½ cups water in saucepan. Bring to boil and simmer 10 minutes. Strain, reserving liquid; discard coconut.

Egyptian Buttermilk Chicken Casserole

        1 broiler-fryer, about 3½ pounds
    1½ cups buttermilk
        2 cloves garlic, crushed
        1 tablespoon curry powder
        2 onions, sliced
        2 tablespoons oil
        1 teaspoon salt
        1 teaspoon sugar
      ¼ teaspoon pepper
        2 teaspoons minced fresh ginger *or*
          ½ teaspoon powdered

Marinate the chicken in buttermilk, garlic, and curry for several hours. Sauté the onions in oil in a casserole; add seasonings. When onions are lightly browned, stir in the buttermilk and add the chicken. Bake at 350°, covered, for about an hour, until the chicken is tender. Reseason to taste. Serve with rice or pilaf, if you wish. Makes 4 servings.

Moroccan Chicken

> 3 onions, sliced
> 2 cloves garlic, minced
> ¼ cup vegetable oil
> 2 teaspoons minced fresh ginger
> 2 teaspoons powdered coriander
> 2 tablespoons minced parsley
> 1 teaspoon salt
> ¼ teaspoon pepper
> 2 broiler-fryers, about 3 pounds *each*, cut up
> 1½ cups chicken broth
> Juice of 1 lemon
> 1 cup pitted or stuffed green olives

Sauté the onion and garlic in oil until transparent but not brown. Combine the ginger, coriander, parsley, salt and pepper and stir in. Add the chicken a few pieces at a time to brown evenly. Add broth and simmer, covered, for half an hour. Add the lemon juice and olives and simmer 15 minutes more until the chicken is tender. Makes 6 servings.

CHINESE COOKING

Chinese cooking is not only one of the oldest, but one of the greatest and most varied cuisines in the world. In Oriental dishes the sauce is very important; it is not served on the side or poured over the finished dish, but is an integral part of the recipe. Usually it includes light or dark soy sauce, and/or Chinese molasses. The ingredients are diced, sliced or slivered into pieces that can easily be lifted with chopsticks. A wok is appropriate for most dishes but an iron skillet is satisfactory; a steamer is also useful. Don't hesitate to try Oriental recipes. Cooking Chinese or Japanese chicken can be a quick, economical and rewarding experience.

Japanese and Chinese soy sauce and other sauces such as oyster, duck and *hoisin* are available in Oriental markets.

*Chop Suey

2 medium onions, minced
3 stalks celery, slivered
3 tablespoons peanut *or* vegetable oil
1 cup shredded Chinese cabbage
2 cups julienned strips of cooked chicken
1 can (5 ounces) bamboo shoots, slivered
1½ cups chicken broth
3 tablespoons soy sauce
1 can (3 ounces) water chestnuts, sliced thin
1 can (1 pound) beansprouts, drained, *or*
1 pound fresh
3 tablespoons cornstarch blended with
3 tablespoons water
Hot cooked rice

Sauté or stir-fry the onions and celery gently in oil for 4 to 5 minutes, until onions are transparent but not brown. Add the remaining ingredients except cornstarch and rice and sauté for 3 minutes. Add the cornstarch and cook until thickened. Serve with rice. Makes 6 servings.

*Easy Chop Suey

1½ cups chicken broth
2 cups sliced celery
2 cups cooked chicken, diced or slivered
1 can (1 pound) beansprouts
4 scallions, slivered
2 tablespoons soy sauce
1 tablespoon cornstarch blended with 2 tablespoons
cold broth or water
1 jar (4 ounces) pimientos, cut into strips
Hot cooked rice

Heat the broth and simmer the celery for 7 minutes. Add the next 4 ingredients and simmer 5 minutes. Stir in the cornstarch. Cook, stirring, until thickened and clear. Add pimientos, reseason, and reheat. Serve with rice. Makes 4 servings.

*Chicken Chow Mein

  6 scallions, slivered
  4 stalks celery, chopped fine
  1 large green pepper, seeded and chopped fine
  2 tablespoons peanut *or* vegetable oil
  ½ pound mushrooms, sliced thin
  3 tablespoons soy sauce
  2 cups chicken broth
  ½ teaspoon salt
  ¼ teaspoon pepper
  3 cups diced cooked chicken
  1 can (1 pound) beansprouts
  1 can (3 ounces) water chestnuts, sliced thin
  3 tablespoons cornstarch blended with
      3 tablespoons water
  Chinese fried noodles

Sauté or stir-fry the scallions, celery and green pepper in oil until light brown. Add the mushrooms and cook 2 minutes. Stir in the soy sauce combined with the broth. Season with salt and pepper. (You need very little salt because of the soy sauce.) Add the chicken, beansprouts and water chestnuts and heat 5 minutes. Stir in the cornstarch and simmer until thickened and clear. Serve with the noodles. Makes 6 servings.

Chinese Chicken

> 6 chicken breasts
> ¼ cup peanut oil *or* part butter
> 1 cup sliced celery
> 1 cup sliced bamboo shoots
> 1 cup sliced water chestnuts
> 1 clove garlic, minced
> ¼ cup soy sauce
> 2 cups chicken broth
> 1 teaspoon salt
> ½ teaspoon pepper
> 1 teaspoon agi no moto *or* monosodium glutamate
> ½ teaspoon ginger
> 2 tablespoons cornstarch blended with a little
>   broth or water
> 1 cup almonds, blanched
> Hot cooked rice

Cut the chicken meat into match-size slivers and cook gently in oil until the chicken turns white, not brown—about 5 minutes. Add the remaining ingredients except the last 3 and heat together for 5 minutes only. Stir in the cornstarch and cook a few minutes until thickened. Sprinkle with almonds (which may be slivered and sautéed gently in a little butter if you like). Serve with rice. Makes 6 to 8 servings.

Easy Chinese Chicken

> 1 broiler-fryer, about 3 pounds, cut up
> ½ cup water
> ⅓ cup soy sauce
> 2 tablespoons oyster sauce *or hoisin* sauce
> ½ teaspoon monosodium glutamate
> Hot cooked rice

Place the chicken in a Dutch oven or other heavy pot and add other ingredients except the rice. Cover and simmer for 40 minutes or until the chicken is tender. Serve with rice. Makes 4 servings.

Chinese Lemon Chicken

> 2 tablespoons soy sauce
> 2 whole chicken breasts, boned
> 2 teaspoons salt
> ½ cup flour
> ¼ cup cornstarch
> Water
> Oil for frying, preferably peanut
> 3 scallions, slivered
> ⅔ cup chicken broth
> 2 teaspoons sugar
> 1 tablespoon lemon juice

Pour soy sauce over the chicken and sprinkle with 1 teaspoon salt. Combine the flour and 2 tablespoons cornstarch, add enough water to make a thin batter, beat well and coat the chicken with this batter. Fry the chicken in hot oil for about 10 minutes, until light brown. Remove and set aside. Put 2 tablespoons of the oil in a skillet or, if using a wok for the frying, pour off all but about 2 tablespoons oil. Fry the scallions for 2 minutes in oil. Add the chicken broth which has been mixed with remaining cornstarch, remaining salt, sugar, and lemon juice. Bring to a boil. Cut the chicken into 1″ pieces, add to the sauce and reheat for 5 minutes. Makes 4 servings.

Chinese Chicken with Wine

> 2 tablespoons vegetable oil
> 1 clove garlic, minced
> 1 broiler-fryer, about 3 pounds, cut up
> 1 cup soy sauce
> 1 cup water
> ¼ cup sugar
> 1 teaspoon minced fresh ginger *or*
>   ½ teaspoon powdered
> ¼ cup dry white wine

Heat oil in Dutch oven or heavy kettle, add garlic and chicken and cook, turning, until chicken is browned evenly on all sides. Add soy sauce, water, sugar, ginger and wine. Cover and simmer, turning occasionally, 45 minutes, or until chicken is tender. Makes 4 servings.

Mandarin Broiled Chicken

> 2 broiler-fryers, 3 to 3½ pounds *each*, cut up
> ½ cup soy sauce
> ¼ cup orange juice
> ¼ cup lemon juice
> ¼ cup vegetable oil
> 1 cup chopped onion
> 1 tablespoon *each* curry and chili powders
> 2 teaspoons monosodium glutamate

Put chicken in shallow dish. Mix remaining ingredients and pour over chicken. Marinate in refrigerator, turning occasionally, at least 2 hours. Drain chicken, reserving marinade, and arrange on broiler pan. Broil about 6" from heat, basting once or twice with marinade, 20 minutes on each side, or until tender and browned. Makes 6 to 8 servings.

Chinese Chicken and Pork

　　1 large onion, chopped
　　2 cloves garlic, minced
　½ green pepper, chopped
　　2 tablespoons peanut *or* vegetable oil
　　1 fryer, about 3 pounds, cut up
1½ pounds lean pork, cut into 1″ cubes
　　1 can (4 ounces) water chestnuts, sliced
　　1 cup water
　½ cup soy sauce
　¼ cup rice wine vinegar
　　　Hot cooked rice

Sauté the onion, garlic and pepper in oil until onion is transparent but not brown. Add the chicken and pork and stir and cook until lightly brown. Add the rest of the ingredients except the rice. Cover and simmer for 40 minutes. Serve with hot rice. Makes 6 servings.

Chinese Chicken with Lettuce

6 slices bacon, cut up
2 tablespoons butter
2 chicken breasts, cut into thin strips
6 scallions, slivered
　Juice and slivered rind of ½ lemon
1 large head Boston lettuce, cut into thin strips
2 tablespoons rice wine vinegar
½ teaspoon sugar

Cook the bacon until crisp; remove pieces, drain and set aside. Add butter to bacon drippings and sauté the chicken for 3 minutes while stirring. Remove and put with bacon pieces. Sauté the scallions 2 minutes, add lemon juice and rind and the lettuce. Cook and stir only until the lettuce starts to wilt. Return chicken and bacon to pan. Add the vinegar and sugar and reheat. Makes 4 to 6 servings.

Cold Chinese Broiled Chicken

> 4 broilers, split, 2 to 2½ pounds *each*
> 1 cup soy sauce
> 1 cup sake *or* sweet sherry
> 2 cloves garlic, crushed
> 2 tablespoons minced fresh ginger
> 2 tablespoons peanut *or* vegetable oil

Put the chicken in a shallow bowl. Combine remaining ingredients and pour over the chicken. Let marinate for several hours, turning to coat all sides. Broil, skin side down, for 20 minutes. Turn, brush with marinade and broil 20 minutes. Remove, cool and chill. You may prefer to serve the chicken at room temperature. Recommended for picnics. Makes 8 servings.

Short-Cut Chinese Chicken

> ½ cup water
> ¼ cup soy sauce
> 3 tablespoons oil
> 2 tablespoons *hoisin* sauce
> 1 broiler-fryer, 2½ to 3 pounds, cut up
> Hot cooked rice

In Dutch oven combine water, soy sauce, oil and *hoisin* sauce. Add chicken and heat to boiling. Reduce heat, cover and simmer 45 minutes or until chicken is tender, turning chicken at least once during cooking. Serve with rice. Makes 4 servings.

Cantonese Chicken

    1 can (4 ounces) water chestnuts
    1 can (4 ounces) bamboo shoots
    1 can (4 ounces) button mushrooms
    3 tablespoons vegetable oil
    1 broiler-fryer, 2½ to 3 pounds, quartered
    1 clove garlic, crushed
    1 medium onion, sliced
    6 pitted prunes
    2 tablespoons cornstarch *or* flour
    ¼ cup soy sauce
    1 tablespoon brown sugar
    ½ teaspoon salt
    ¼ teaspoon ginger
    ¼ cup sherry

Drain liquids from first 3 ingredients and add enough water to make 1½ cups; reserve. Heat oil in large skillet, add chicken and brown on both sides. Add garlic and sauté a few minutes. Put in 2½-quart casserole. Add water chestnuts, bamboo shoots, mushrooms, onion and prunes. Mix remaining ingredients until smooth. Add to reserved liquid and pour over chicken mixture. Bake, uncovered, at 400° for about 50 minutes. Makes 4 servings.

Chinese-Noodle Chicken

    ¼ cup butter *or* margarine, melted
    1 tablespoon soy sauce
    1 tablespoon lemon juice
    1 broiler-fryer, about 3 pounds, cut up, *or* 4 *each*
        chicken thighs and drumsticks
    1 can (3 ounces) Chinese noodles, finely crushed

Mix first 3 ingredients and brush on chicken. Coat with noodles and put on lightly oiled foil-lined shallow pan. Bake at 400° 1 hour, or until well browned. Makes 4 servings.

Easy Oriental Chicken

    1 fryer, about 3 pounds, cut up
    ½ cup peanut oil
    ¼ cup honey
    1 cup soy sauce
    ¼ teaspoon ginger
    ½ cup minced chives *or* scallions
    1 clove garlic, crushed

Put the chicken in a bowl. Combine remaining ingredients. When well blended, pour over the chicken and let stand for 3 or 4 hours. Place chicken and the marinade in a baking dish and bake, covered, at 350° for 45 minutes. Uncover and put under the broiler for 5 minutes, or turn oven up to 500° for the last 5 minutes of baking. Good with rice or fried rice. Makes 4 servings.

*Chicken with an Oriental Flavor

    2 cups diced cooked chicken meat
    3 teaspoons cornstarch
    1 tablespoon dry sherry
    ¼ teaspoon monosodium glutamate
      Salt to taste
    ⅓ cup cold water
    ¼ cup vegetable oil
    1 clove garlic, crushed
    1 can (6 ounces) diced bamboo shoots, drained
    1 can (4 ounces) diced water chestnuts, drained
    2 medium green peppers, diced

Mix chicken, 1 teaspoon cornstarch, the sherry, monosodium glutamate and salt; set aside. Blend remaining cornstarch and the cold water and set aside. Pour oil into hot skillet over medium-high heat. Add garlic, then stir in chicken mixture. Cook, stirring, 2 minutes (a stiff spatula makes a good tool for stirring).

Add bamboo shoots and water chestnuts, stir 1 minute, then add green pepper and mix well. Add cornstarch mixture and cook, stirring, until thickened. Serve at once. Makes 4 servings.

Chicken with Oriental Vegetables

> 1 can (4 ounces) mushrooms *or* ⅛ pound dried mushrooms soaked in ½ cup water
> ¼ cup soy sauce
> ¼ cup water
> 3 teaspoons cornstarch
> 1 teaspoon minced fresh ginger *or* ¼ teaspoon powdered
> ¼ cup peanut *or* other vegetable oil
> 2 pounds boneless chicken breasts, cut in thin strips
> 1 cup slivered celery
> 1 cup slivered scallions
> 1 can (1 pound) beansprouts, drained
> 1 can (5 ounces) water chestnuts, drained and sliced thin
> Cooked rice

If using dried mushrooms, soak them at least an hour. Drain the mushrooms and combine the liquid with next four ingredients. Slice the mushrooms. Heat the oil in a wok or heavy skillet, add the chicken and stir-fry only until it turns white, 3 or 4 minutes. Add the celery, scallions and mushrooms and cook 2 minutes. Pour in the liquid, add beansprouts and water chestnuts and stir-cook 3 or 4 minutes, until heated through. Serve with rice. Makes 6 servings.

Chicken Sukiyaki

>½ pound mushrooms, sliced
>3 tablespoons peanut *or* vegetable oil
>1 large green pepper, diced *or* slivered
>4 scallions, slivered
>2 stalks celery, scraped and slivered
>⅓ cup soy sauce
>½ cup chicken broth
>1 can (6 ounces) water chestnuts, sliced
>2 pounds boneless chicken breasts, sliced thin
>Hot cooked rice

Brown the mushrooms in oil for 2 minutes; add the remaining ingredients, except rice, placing the chicken on top. Simmer for 10 to 15 minutes, until the chicken turns white. The vegetables should be crisp. This is effective cooked at the table in a chafing dish or iron skillet. Serve with rice. Makes 6 servings.

*Quick Japanese Chicken with Sesame

>3 tablespoons butter
>3 tablespoons flour
>1½ cups chicken broth
>1 clove garlic, crushed
>3 cups diced cooked chicken
>1 tablespoon soy sauce
>2 tablespoons sesame seeds
>3 cups cooked rice

Melt the butter in a casserole, blend in the flour, and pour in the broth slowly while stirring. When smooth, add garlic, chicken, and soy sauce. Add the sesame seeds and spread rice over the top. Cover and cook until heated through, about 10 minutes. Makes 6 servings.

15 *Kebabs*

Food on skewers—kebabs or brochettes—is popular everywhere. Kebabs are ideal for entertaining, since they may be made long ahead of time. If they are made ahead, the ingredients may be strung on a skewer, brushed with a marinade, folded in foil and placed in the refrigerator. From there they go directly to the broiler and, some fifteen minutes later, to the plate of each guest, who will exclaim over the attractive arrangement of chicken and vegetables. If they are to be cooked soon they do not have to be refrigerated or even marinated.

In the Near East, where they are called kebabs, the spelling varies a great deal. In India, they are *tandoori;* in Singapore, they are called *satay;* in Russia, *shaslik;* in France, where they are more elegant, the title is *brochette.* In Japan, they are *yakitori,* and only one kind of chicken part is put on a skewer at a time—breasts, legs, thighs, wings, gizzards or livers. We like to combine them; but either way, and by any name, kebabs are delicious, colorful, reasonable and a conversation piece.

Greek Chicken Kebabs

½ cup olive oil
⅓ cup lemon juice
1 clove garlic, crushed
1 teaspoon salt
¼ teaspoon pepper
½ teaspoon basil *or* rosemary
½ teaspoon oregano
3 whole chicken breasts, skinned, boned and cut
   into 1″ cubes
1 pound small white onions, parboiled
2 large green peppers, seeded and cut into 1½″ squares
3 green tomatoes, quartered
Wheat pilaf *or* rice

Combine the oil, lemon juice, garlic, salt, pepper, basil or rosemary, and oregano. Add the chicken and marinate several hours. Alternate chicken, onions, pepper squares, and tomato quarters on 6 long skewers. Brush with marinade and broil 10 minutes, turn, brush again and broil 10 minutes more. Pour marinade over and serve with bulgur (cracked wheat) pilaf or rice. Makes 6 servings.

Turkish Chicken Shish Kebab

     Lemon juice *or* vinegar
½ cup red wine
1 teaspoon salt
½ teaspoon pepper
1 bay leaf, crushed
     Pinch of oregano
¼ cup water
4 chicken breasts, skinned, boned and cut into 1" cubes
1 onion, chopped
1 clove garlic, crushed
1 eggplant
1 can (1 pound) artichoke bottoms
2 green peppers, seeded and cut in eighths
16 cherry tomatoes
¼ cup olive oil
     Hot wheat pilaf *or* rice

Mix ¼ cup lemon juice, the wine, ½ teaspoon salt, ¼ teaspoon pepper, the bay leaf, oregano and ¼ cup water in saucepan. Bring to boil and simmer 2 minutes. Pour over combined chicken, onion and garlic. Leave several hours or overnight. Peel eggplant, cut in 1½" slices and quarter each slice. Alternate chicken, eggplant, artichoke bottoms, pepper pieces and tomatoes on skewers. Brush with the oil mixed with 1 tablespoon lemon juice and marinade. Sprinkle with remaining salt and pepper and broil 8 to 10 minutes, turning once and basting with marinade mixture. Serve with wheat pilaf or with brown or white rice. Makes 8 servings.

Italian Chicken Kebabs

   3 chicken breasts, skinned, boned and cut into
      24 pieces
   2 tablespoons lemon juice
   1 teaspoon salt
   ½ teaspoon pepper
   ¼ teaspoon thyme
   ½ pound Swiss cheese, cut into 24 long pieces
   ½ pound prosciutto *or* other ham, cut into
      24 long pieces
   6 tomatoes, quartered
   2 tablespoons olive oil

Season the chicken with lemon juice, salt, pepper and thyme. Wrap each piece of chicken in cheese and prosciutto. Alternate these rolls with tomato quarters on 6 skewers. Just before broiling, brush with oil. Broil 10 minutes, turn, baste with oil, and broil 5 minutes more. Makes 6 servings.

Japanese Yakitori I

   2½ pounds drumsticks, thighs, breasts *or* wings
   ⅓ cup soy sauce
   ¾ cup sake *or* sweet sherry
   1 to 2 tablespoons sugar
   1 tablespoon peanut *or* vegetable oil
   Hot cooked rice *or* pilaf

Cut breasts or thighs into a total of about 24 pieces. If you use wings or small drumsticks, leave them whole. String the chicken on 12 small or 6 large metal skewers. Combine remaining ingredients, except rice. Place skewers on foil, pour sauce over, fold the foil and refrigerate several hours. (If you wish to cook and serve at once, omit last step and simply dip the skewers in the sauce.) Broil for 10 minutes, dip again or brush with sauce, turn and broil 10 minutes more. Serve with remaining sauce on the side for dipping. Serve with rice or pilaf. Makes 6 servings.

Japanese Yakitori II

    1½ to 2 pounds chicken breasts (with bone)
    ½ pound chicken livers
    ½ cup soy sauce
    ¼ cup sweet sherry *or* sake
    2 tablespoons sugar

Cut chicken breasts and livers in ½" to ¾" pieces. Thread on short skewers. Dip in sauce made by combining remaining ingredients. Broil on one side for 10 minutes, dip again in sauce and broil on other side. Dip once more in sauce before serving. Good served with rice. Makes 4 to 6 regular or 12 canapé servings.

Tandoori

    3 tablespoons lemon juice
    1 pint yogurt
    1 teaspoon salt
    ¼ teaspoon pepper
    ½ teaspoon cayenne
    ½ teaspoon powdered ginger
    ½ teaspoon ground coriander
    2 broiler-fryers, 2½ to 3 pounds *each,* cut up
    3 not-too-ripe tomatoes, quartered
    2 tablespoons vegetable *or* olive oil

Combine the lemon juice with the yogurt. Season with salt, pepper, cayenne, ginger and coriander. Rub the chicken with the mixture. String on 6 long or 12 short skewers, alternating with the tomato wedges. When ready to broil, brush with oil and broil for

15 minutes. Turn, brush with oil and any remaining yogurt mixture, and broil 10 minutes more.

Singapore Satay

>   2 large chicken breasts, skinned and boned
>   2 tablespoons *each* lemon juice and soy sauce
>   ¼ cup coconut milk (see page 212) *or* evaporated milk
>   2 tablespoons olive oil
>   1 tablespoon ground coriander
>   1 tablespoon brown sugar
>   ½ teaspoon turmeric
>   1 teaspoon caraway seed
>   1 teaspoon instant minced onion
>   1 clove garlic, crushed (optional)
>   ½ teaspoon salt
>   ¼ teaspoon pepper
>   ¼ teaspoon paprika *or* cayenne
>   3 tablespoons peanut butter

Cut meat in ½" to ¾" cubes and put in bowl. Bring remaining ingredients to boil. Pour over meat and marinate several hours. Then thread meat on small bamboo skewers or short metal ones and broil about 3 minutes on each side. For a quick, easy way to make satay, broil meat sprinkled with salt and pepper and dip in sauce before serving; pass remaining sauce. Makes 6 regular servings or 12 canapé servings.

Iranian Chelo Kabâb

    3 pounds chicken breasts, ground
    3 medium onions, grated or ground fine
      Salt
      Pepper
      Few drops of lemon juice
      Saffron
    9 to 11 egg yolks, all but 3 in half shells
    1 pound long-grain rice
      Water
    2 tablespoons vegetable oil
    6 to 8 pats butter
      Paprika *or* ground chilies (optional)

Put meat in bowl and cover with grated onion. Refrigerate several hours. Half an hour before cooking, scrape off onions. Add 1 teaspoon salt, ¼ teaspoon pepper, the lemon juice, ½ teaspoon saffron and 2 egg yolks; mix thoroughly. Make 6 long flat patties. Wet skewers and shape meat around in cylinders. Seal edges and be sure meat is tight—it should not come quite to ends. Broil, turning once or twice to brown all sides. Do not overcook—a few minutes is enough. Meanwhile, pour rice and 3 tablespoons salt into 4 quarts boiling water. Boil 8 to 10 minutes, or until center of grain is just soft. Drain and rinse with cool or warm water. Heat oil with 2 tablespoons water in 3-quart heat-proof casserole. Mix ½ cup rice with an egg yolk (not in shell) and spread over bottom of casserole. Add remaining rice, piling in center. Cover and bake at 350° for 30 minutes. Turn out on warm serving dish, scraping browned part over top. Serve with butter pats and egg yolks in half shells. Each person makes a well in his helping of rice and drops in a butter pat, an egg yolk and a little salt and pepper to taste. Serve with kabâbs. In Iran a red condiment, an edible sumac, is added. This is not the kind available in this country; we can substitute a little saffron, paprika or ground chilies. Makes 6 to 8 servings.

Chicken Brochette

6 whole chicken breasts
White wine
1 cup minced green onions, with tops
1 tablespoon turmeric
1 teaspoon paprika
⅓ cup olive oil
Salt and pepper to taste
1 pound mushrooms
Cherry tomatoes

Remove skin from chicken breasts. Bone by cutting off meat with point of sharp knife; cut meat in fairly large pieces. Put in large bowl and add enough wine to cover. Add remaining ingredients, except mushrooms and tomatoes. Marinate, turning now and then, 1 to 2 hours. String chicken on skewers, alternating with mushrooms and tomatoes. Grill over prepared coals or in oven broiler, turning once, until tender. Baste with marinade before and during cooking. Serve on skewers. Makes 8 servings.

French Chicken Livers en Brochette

1 pound chicken livers
4 slices bacon
1 teaspoon salt
¼ teaspoon pepper
¼ teaspoon oregano

Cut the livers into 3 or 4 pieces each. Cut the bacon in squares. Alternate liver and bacon on 4 large or 8 small skewers. Sprinkle with salt, pepper, and oregano. Put on a rack in a baking pan and bake at 425° until bacon is crisp. Makes 4 servings.

Swiss Chicken-Liver Brochettes

> 2 pounds chicken livers, halved
> 1 teaspoon salt
> ¼ teaspoon pepper
> ½ teaspoon thyme, sage *or* poultry seasoning
> ½ to ¾ pound bacon

Sprinkle the chicken livers with salt, pepper and herb. Cut the pieces of bacon in half and fold around the livers. String on 6 long skewers, leaving a little space between the pieces so the bacon can brown. Broil for 5 minutes, turn and broil 3 or 4 minutes more until the bacon is crisp. Good served with rice. Makes 6 servings.

Mushroom Chicken Kebabs

> 1 pound small mushrooms
> 2 large chicken breasts, skinned, boned and cut
>   into 1" pieces
> 1 teaspoon salt
> ½ teaspoon garlic salt
> ½ teaspoon oregano
> 2 tablespoons oil *or* melted butter
> Minced chives

Trim the stems and parboil the mushrooms for 1 minute—this ensures their not splitting when you string them on skewers. String them on the skewers, alternating with pieces of chicken. Sprinkle with a mixture of salt, garlic salt and oregano. Brush with oil or butter and broil 7 minutes, turn and broil 5 minutes more. Sprinkle with the chives. Makes 6 servings.

PART IV

Soups,
Sandwiches,
Salads

16 *The Three S's:*
Soups, Sandwiches
and Salads

SOUPS

Nothing is easier to cook than soup, which can survive even the proverbial "too many cooks." One can boil it down or add liquids, toss in herbs, spices and leftovers, and even subtract salt (by means of a slice of raw potato, subsequently removed). So feel free to take liberties with the following recipes.

Thin soups can precede a hearty meal while robust ones can be a meal in themselves. With the aid of a blender, low-calorie thick soups are easily prepared. But thick or thin, chicken broth is the priceless ingredient of many good soups—priceless in both senses of the word, for it can be made from the carcass of a roaster, the liquid (left over after making gravy) in which a hen was fricasseed, or the backs, necks and gizzards saved for that purpose or bought very inexpensively. And if you don't happen to have any chicken broth in your refrigerator or freezer, there's nothing wrong with using canned broth or mixes.

Chicken Broth I

    1 stewing chicken, about 4 pounds
    8 cups cold water
    2 stalks celery with leaves, cut up
    1 onion, cut up
    3 sprigs parsley
    8 peppercorns
    1 teaspoon salt

Put the chicken, including giblets, in a heavy, deep pot with the
remaining ingredients. Cover and simmer about 2½ hours, until
the chicken is tender. Remove chicken. Strain broth, discarding
vegetables. Cool, and skim off the fat. The chicken can be used
in recipes for leftovers. Yield: about 6 cups.

Chicken Broth II

Substitute 4 to 5 pounds of chicken backs, necks, wings and feet
(if available) for the whole chicken and proceed as for Chicken
Broth I.

Chicken Broth III

Use a leftover carcass and any skin and scraps of chicken. Cover
with cold water and proceed as for Chicken Broth I, cooking the
soup for 1 hour.

Herbed Chicken Broth

        5 to 6 cups chicken broth
        ½ cup chopped celery leaves
        ¼ cup chopped onion
        3 sprigs parsley
        1 bay leaf
        3 whole cloves
        ½ teaspoon tarragon
        ½ teaspoon thyme
        1 carrot, diced
           Salt and pepper to taste

Bring all of the ingredients, except salt and pepper, to a boil and simmer, covered, for half an hour. Strain. Add salt and pepper to taste. The amount of seasoning will depend upon the seasoning in the broth. Makes 6 servings.

Chicken Consommé Rosé

Add 2 cups of tomato juice to 6 cups of chicken broth with ½ teaspoon sugar and some minced parsley. Makes 8 servings.

Lemon Chicken Broth

Add 3 tablespoons lemon juice beaten with 2 eggs to 6 cups of chicken broth. Heat, but do not boil. Makes 6 servings.

*Japanese Chicken Broth with Vegetables

    5 cups strong chicken broth
    ½ cup small pieces cooked chicken
    ¼ cup slivered fresh green beans
    ¼ cup diced water chestnuts
    1 green onion, thinly sliced
      Salt and pepper to taste

Heat broth and add the chicken and vegetables; season to taste.
Simmer a few minutes. Makes about 6 servings.

Cream of Chicken Soup

    5 cups of chicken broth, homemade or canned
    1 cup minced celery
    3 tablespoons butter
    3 tablespoons flour
    1 cup heavy cream
      Salt to taste

Put the broth in a large pot with the celery. Cover and simmer
until the celery is very tender. Whirl in a blender. Melt the butter, stir in the flour and add 1 cup of broth slowly while stirring.
Return to the pot with remaining broth and simmer 5 minutes.
Add the cream and heat but don't boil. Add salt to taste. Makes
6 servings.

*Easy Curried Cream of Chicken Soup

1 stalk celery, diced
1 small onion, minced
2 tablespoons butter *or* margarine
1 teaspoon curry powder
1 cup minced chicken
2 cans (10½ ounces *each*) cream of chicken soup
2 soup-cans milk
Toasted slivered almonds *or* coconut

Sauté celery and onion in the butter in saucepan 2 to 3 minutes. Stir in curry powder, chicken, then soup and milk. Heat, stirring. Serve with a garnish of almonds or coconut. Makes 4 servings.

*Chicken Bisque

2 tablespoons butter
2 tablespoons flour
3 cups seasoned chicken broth
1 cup finely diced cooked chicken
1 cup milk
Chopped chives, seasoned salt and white pepper
to taste

Melt butter in saucepan and blend in flour. Gradually add broth and cook, stirring, until slightly thickened. Whirl chicken with the milk in blender until finely minced. Add to soup and heat. Add seasonings. Makes 4 servings.

Italian Rice Soup with Chicken Livers

    ½ cup raw rice
    1 tablespoon butter *or* margarine
    4 cups chicken broth
      Salt and pepper
    6 chicken livers, cooked
    1 egg yolk
      Chopped parsley
      Grated Parmesan cheese

Lightly brown rice in the butter in saucepan. Add broth, bring to boil and season with salt and pepper. Cover and simmer until rice is done. Meanwhile, chop livers and mix with beaten egg yolk. Remove rice from heat and add liver mixture. Serve in bowls with a sprinkling of parsley and grated cheese. Makes 4 servings.

Chicken and Matzo-Ball Soup

    1 stewing chicken, 4 to 5 pounds
    2 ribs celery, cut up
    2 large carrots, cut up
  1½ teaspoons salt
  10 peppercorns
    1 bay leaf
    2 quarts water
      Matzo Balls (see following)

In covered kettle simmer all ingredients except Matzo Balls 2 to 3 hours or until chicken is very tender. Remove chicken and strain broth, discarding vegetables. (Pull chicken from bones to use in another soup, or in sandwiches, salad or other recipes.) Return broth to kettle, cover and chill. Lift off and reserve fat for Matzo Balls. To serve, bring to boil, drop Matzo Balls into boiling broth and simmer about 10 minutes. Makes 6 servings.

Matzo Balls

> ½ cup water
> 2 heaping tablespoons solid chicken fat (about
>   3 tablespoons melted) from broth
> ¾ teaspoon salt, or to taste
>   Pepper to taste
> ¾ cup matzo meal
> 2 eggs

In small saucepan heat water to boiling. Stir in chicken fat to melt, salt and pepper. Quickly stir in matzo meal and remove from heat. Cool 5 minutes. Add eggs and mix well. Refrigerate until well chilled, at least 1 hour. Pinch off golf-ball-size pieces and roll between wet hands. Makes 6 balls.

Chicken-Vegetable Soup with Dumplings

> 1 stewing chicken, 4 to 5 pounds
>   Water
> 2 teaspoons salt
> 1 tablespoon cider vinegar
> 1 bay leaf
> 1 onion, quartered
>   Celery tops and leaves
> 1 cup *each* thinly sliced carrots and celery
> 1 cup frozen peas
>   Dumplings (see page 139)
>   Chopped parsley (optional)

Put chicken in large heavy kettle or Dutch oven. Add water to cover, bring to boil and boil rapidly 15 minutes. Skim, then add next 5 ingredients. Cover and simmer 3 hours, or until meat falls from bones. Remove chicken, discard skin and bones and reserve meat for another use. Strain broth (there will be about 8 cups), boil and add remaining vegetables. Drop dumpling batter by teaspoonfuls into boiling soup, cover, reduce heat and simmer 10 minutes. Sprinkle with parsley, if desired. Makes 8 servings.

Chicken-Noodle Soup
(*Make the day before*)

      2 quarts water
      1 stewing chicken with giblets, 3 to 4 pounds, cut up
      1 medium onion
        Few parsley sprigs
      1 teaspoon peppercorns
        Salt
      6 ounces egg noodles
      1 cup diced celery
      ½ cup shredded carrot
      ½ teaspoon *each* thyme and oregano

Bring water to boil in kettle or Dutch oven with chicken, giblets, onion, parsley, peppercorns and 1 teaspoon salt. Simmer, covered, 3 hours, or until chicken is tender. Remove chicken and cool. Strain broth into bowl. Cool, then refrigerate. Next day, lift off fat and put broth in kettle. Remove skin and bones from chicken and dice meat and giblets. Bring broth to boil and add salt to taste and remaining ingredients. Bring again to boil and cook, partially covered, stirring occasionally, 10 minutes, or until noodles are tender. Add chicken and heat. Makes about 8 servings.

Chicken-Noodle Soup with Red Beans

     3 pounds chicken parts—backs, necks and wings
     2 quarts water
     2 stalks celery, cut up
       Celery leaves
     2 sprigs parsley
     1 onion, cut up
     1 cup shredded cabbage
     1 carrot, cut up
     1 teaspoon salt
   ½ teaspoon pepper
     1 pound pork sausage
     1 can (10½ ounces) vegetable soup
     1 can (1 pound 4 ounces) kidney beans
     1 cup broken-up uncooked fine noodles

Put the chicken pieces in a large pot with water; add the next 8
ingredients. Bring to a boil and simmer for about 2 hours or until
the chicken is very tender. Remove the chicken and pick the meat
off the bones. Strain the broth. Sauté the sausage until brown,
breaking it up with a fork. Put the sausage and chicken into the
broth with the vegetable soup, kidney beans and noodles. Simmer
for 10 to 12 minutes, until noodles are tender. Makes 8 servings.

*Chicken-Rice Soup

     3 tablespoons chicken fat *or* oil
     1 cup sliced carrot
     1 cup *each* chopped celery and onion
     6 cups chicken broth
   ¼ cup rice
     2 teaspoons salt
       Freshly ground pepper
     1 cup cooked chicken, cut in bite-size
         pieces (optional)

Heat fat in kettle or Dutch oven and sauté carrot, celery and onion 10 minutes. Add broth and bring to boil. Stir in rice, salt and pepper; cover and simmer 30 minutes. Add chicken and heat through. Taste and correct seasonings. Makes about 6 servings.

Avgolemono
(Greek Chicken-Lemon Soup)

    4 cups chicken broth
    ⅓ cup raw rice
    1 teaspoon salt (preferably sea salt)
    ¼ teaspoon pepper
    3 egg yolks, beaten
    1 to 2 tablespoons lemon juice

Put the broth and rice in a heavy pot. Cover and simmer for 25 to 30 minutes, until the rice is slightly overdone. Add salt and pepper. Combine the egg yolks with 1 tablespoon lemon juice. Spoon some hot sauce into the yolks while stirring and return the mixture to the pot. Heat 2 minutes. Keep stirring and do not boil. Add more salt and lemon juice to taste. Makes 4 servings.

Chicken Soup with Escarole

    2 chicken breasts, split
      Water
    2 teaspoons salt
    3 stalks celery, sliced
    1 medium onion, cut up
    1 can (6 ounces) tomato paste
    ¾ pound ground beef
    1 egg
    ½ cup dry bread crumbs
    1½ pounds escarole
      Grated Parmesan cheese

Put the chicken in a pot with 6 cups of water. Add 1½ teaspoons salt, celery, onion and tomato paste. Simmer 45 minutes, until chicken is tender. Meanwhile, mix the beef with egg, bread crumbs and the remaining salt. With the hands, form into about 18 small balls. Remove chicken and, when cool enough to handle, take the meat off the bones and cut it up. Return to the broth with the meat balls. Cook the escarole in a small amount of water for 5 minutes, chop coarsely and add with the liquid to the broth. Cook for 5 minutes. Serve soup sprinkled with cheese. Makes 6 servings.

Italian Escarole Soup

```
      1 chicken or hen, about 4 pounds
      6 cups water
   1½ teaspoons salt
      ¼ cup tomato puree or ½ cup tomato sauce
      1 clove garlic, crushed
      3 stalks celery, cut up
      ¼ teaspoon pepper
      1 tablespoon minced parsley
      1 cup cracker meal
      ⅓ cup grated Parmesan cheese
      1 egg slightly beaten
   1½ pounds escarole
```

Put the bird in a large pot with water, 1 teaspoon salt, tomato puree, garlic and celery. Simmer until tender, about 1½ hours for a young chicken and up to 3 hours for a hen. Meanwhile, make the balls by combining remaining salt, pepper and parsley with the cracker meal, 2 tablespoons Parmesan cheese, and the egg. Form into about 18 small balls. When chicken is done and cool enough to handle, take meat from the bones and remove skin. Return chicken to the broth. Heat the escarole for 2 or 3 minutes in a little broth. Add to pot with the balls and cook about 10 minutes. Sprinkle with remaining cheese just before serving. Makes 6 servings.

Chicken Soup with Vegetables

    1 broiler-fryer, about 3 pounds, cut up
      Water
    2 teaspoons salt
    4 stalks celery, cut up
    3 carrots, scraped and sliced
    1 can (8 ounces) tomato puree
    1 egg beaten with ¼ cup water
    ½ cup cracker meal
    2 teaspoons chopped parsley
    ½ teaspoon oregano
    1 pound spinach

Simmer the chicken in 6 cups water with 1½ teaspoons salt, celery, carrots and tomato puree for about an hour. Meanwhile, mix remaining salt with the egg-water mixture, the cracker meal, parsley and oregano. Form into small balls. When chicken is done, remove meat from bones, cut up and return to the broth with the balls. Boil the spinach in ½ cup water for 3 minutes. Drain and add to the broth. Simmer 5 minutes. Makes 6 servings.

Chicken Soup with Tomatoes and Chick-Peas

    1 frying chicken, about 3 pounds, cut up
      Water
      Salt
    1 can (17 ounces) chick-peas, undrained
    1 can (1 pound) tomatoes
    1 cup diced potatoes
    ¼ cup chopped onion
    1 tablespoon minced parsley *or* parsley flakes
    ¼ teaspoon ginger
    2 tablespoons white wine

Put chicken in a kettle and add 4 cups water, or enough to cover chicken. Season with salt, bring to boil, cover and simmer until chicken is very tender. Remove from broth and take meat from bones. Put meat back in broth and add remaining ingredients except the wine. Bring again to a boil and simmer about 15 minutes, until potatoes are tender. Add wine and serve in bowls. Makes 6 servings.

*Special Chicken Soup

    2 cups diced cooked chicken
    3 cups diced cooked potatoes
    1 package (10 ounces) frozen corn
    5 cups chicken broth
      Salt and pepper to taste
    1 cup heavy cream

Simmer the chicken, potatoes and corn in the broth with salt and pepper for 10 to 12 minutes. Add the cream and adjust seasoning. The amount of salt depends upon the seasoning in the chicken broth. Reheat. Makes 6 servings.

*Chicken Soup with Celery Root

    1 medium celery root, peeled and cut up
      Water
    2 cans (10½ ounces *each*) cream of chicken soup
    1 cup cooked diced chicken
    1 cup half-and-half
      Salt and pepper
      Minced celery leaves

Put the celery root in a pot with water to cover and simmer until tender. Drain off some of the liquid and whirl the rest with the root in a blender; put back in the saucepan with celery liquid and chicken soup. Heat and stir until smooth. Add chicken and half-

and-half and reheat. Season to taste with salt and pepper and serve with a few celery leaves on top. Makes 6 servings.

Chicken and Chinese-Cabbage Soup

>   1 broiler-fryer, cut up
>   Water
>   2 teaspoons salt
>   5 whole white peppercorns
>   1 onion, quartered
>   1 bay leaf
>   Few parsley sprigs
>   1 small Chinese cabbage, trimmed and cut
>   crosswise in ½" shreds
>   ½ cup sliced radishes *or* water chestnuts *or*
>   chopped parsley

Put chicken, 1 quart water and next 5 ingredients in large saucepan. Bring to boil, reduce heat and simmer 45 minutes; cool. Take chicken from broth, remove skin and bones and cut meat in strips. Strain broth and add enough water to measure 4 cups. Bring to boil, add cabbage and allow to wilt. Add chicken and radishes and correct seasoning. Makes about 6 servings.

Jellied Chicken-Vegetable Soup

>   1 envelope unflavored gelatin
>   Water
>   1 can (10½ ounces) chicken broth
>   ½ teaspoon dry mustard
>   1 teaspoon Worcestershire sauce
>   ½ cup finely grated carrot
>   ¾ cup minced celery
>   ½ cup minced radishes
>   Minced chives *or* green onions

Soften gelatin in ¼ cup cold water. Dissolve over low heat and add to chicken broth with 1 can cold water. Add mustard and Worcestershire, mixed together. Chill to consistency of unbeaten egg white. Then fold in remaining ingredients, except chives. Spoon into 6 individual 5-ounce serving dishes and chill. Sprinkle top with chives. Makes 6 servings.

Chicken Gumbo

    2 broiler-fryers, about 3 pounds *each*, cut up
    2 cups water
    2 medium onions, sliced
    2 bay leaves
    1 teaspoon monosodium glutamate
      Salt
    2 tablespoons butter *or* margarine
    1 medium green pepper, chopped
    2 cans (1 pound *each*) tomatoes
    3 tablespoons chopped parsley
    ¾ cup raw rice
    ½ pound fresh okra, sliced, *or* 1 package
        (10 ounces) frozen
    2 teaspoons filé powder

Wash chicken pieces and put in kettle. Add water, 1 onion, bay leaves, monosodium glutamate and 1 teaspoon salt. Cover and simmer for 45 minutes. Remove from heat; strain broth and return to kettle. Remove meat from bones and cut into bite-size pieces; return to broth. Melt butter, add remaining onion and green pepper, and cook for about 5 minutes. Add to chicken with 1 teaspoon salt, tomatoes and parsley. Simmer for 20 minutes. Add rice and okra; simmer for 20 minutes longer. Remove from heat and stir in filé powder. Do not reheat. Makes 6 to 8 servings.

Chicken Chowder

    1 hen, about 4 pounds, cut up
      Water
    2 teaspoons salt
    3 slices bacon, cut up
    2 medium onions, sliced
    4 large potatoes, peeled and cut in large pieces
    2 cups half-and-half
      Flour (optional)
    2 tablespoons butter

Put the chicken in a Dutch oven with water almost to cover, add
1 teaspoon salt, cover and simmer for about 2 hours, until the
chicken is tender. Remove chicken. Fry the bacon; remove the
pieces and set aside. Brown the onion lightly in bacon fat and put
into the pot the chicken was cooked in. Add potatoes, remaining
salt and 1 cup water. Simmer until potatoes are almost tender,
about 15 minutes. Meanwhile remove meat from the chicken
bones and cut it up. Discard the skin. Put the chicken, bacon bits
and half-and-half into the pot and simmer about 10 minutes.
Thicken, if you wish, with a little flour-and-water paste. Add the
butter just before serving. Makes 6 servings.

Chicken Avocado Soup

    ½ cup minced onion
    1 cup finely chopped celery
    3 tablespoons butter
    2 cups water
    2 cans (10½ ounces *each*) cream of chicken soup
    2 ripe avocados
      Lemon slices

Sauté the onion and celery in butter until the onion is transparent; do not brown. Add water and simmer 10 minutes. Add the

soup and bring to a boil. Peel and sieve, rice or crush the avocados, saving a few slices for garnish. Add this puree to the soup and reheat. (You may chill if you prefer—this soup is good hot or cold.) Serve garnished with avocado and lemon slices. Makes 6 servings.

*Chicken-Celery Soup

    4 cups chicken broth
    2 ribs celery, sliced
    1 cup cooked rice
    1 cup (or more) diced cooked chicken
    2 green onions *or* celery tops, minced
    2 teaspoons lemon juice
      Salt and pepper to taste

Pour broth into saucepan and bring to boil. Add celery and simmer 5 minutes or until crisp-tender. Add rice, chicken and onions and heat just to boiling. Stir in lemon juice. Heat and season with salt and pepper. Makes about 6 servings.

Mulligatawny Soup

    1 apple, peeled and sliced thin
    1 medium onion, sliced thin
    1 carrot, sliced thin
    2 tablespoons butter *or* margarine
    2 tablespoons flour
    2 to 3 teaspoons curry powder
    2 quarts chicken broth
      Juice of ½ lemon
      Hot cooked rice

Sauté apple, onion and carrot in hot butter in skillet. Sprinkle with flour and curry powder and brown thoroughly. Add stock and bring to a boil, stirring. Cover and simmer 30 minutes. Skim out solids and puree in blender or rub through sieve; return to pan and bring to boil. Stir in lemon juice. Serve with rice. Makes about 8 servings.

Short-Cut Mulligatawny Soup

    2 tablespoons butter
    1 tablespoon curry powder
    4 teaspoons flour
      Water
    2 cans (10¾ ounces *each*) chicken broth
    ½ cup heavy cream
      Hot cooked rice

Melt butter in 2-quart saucepan, add curry powder and heat until sizzling. Blend in flour. Add enough water to broth to make 4 cups and stir into hot mixture. Bring to boil, stirring. Add cream and heat but do not boil. Put a few tablespoonfuls rice in each bowl and add soup. Makes about 4 servings.

*Cold Chicken Soup with Curry

    1 medium onion, sliced
    2 apples, cored, peeled and cut up
    1 tablespoon butter
    1 teaspoon flour
    1 tablespoon curry powder
    1 teaspoon salt
    ¼ teaspoon pepper
    3 cups chicken broth
    ½ cup white wine
    ½ cup diced cooked chicken
    2 cups half-and-half

Sauté onion and apple in melted butter until soft. Mix flour with curry, salt and pepper, and cook slowly, stirring, for about 5 minutes. Add broth and wine and cook slowly for 10 minutes, stirring constantly. Rub mixture through a sieve or whirl in blender. Chill. At serving time, add diced chicken and chilled half-and-half. Serve cold. Makes 6 servings.

*Chilled Curried Chicken Soup

      2 cans (10½ ounces *each*) cream of chicken soup
      2 soup-cans milk
      ¼ cup lemon juice
      1 tablespoon curry powder, or to taste
      1 cup minced cooked chicken
        Thin red onion rings

Put soup in mixing bowl and gradually beat in milk until smooth. Add lemon juice and curry powder and beat until well blended. Add chicken. Cover and chill several hours or overnight. Garnish with a few onion rings. Makes 4 servings.

Chilled Chicken-Chutney Soup

      2 cans (10¾ ounces *each*) chicken broth
      1 teaspoon curry powder
      2 tablespoons chopped mango chutney
      2 egg yolks
      ½ cup heavy cream
      ½ teaspoon lemon juice
      3 tablespoons finely diced peeled cucumber
        Toasted flaked *or* shredded coconut (optional)

Put first 3 ingredients in saucepan and bring to boil. Remove from heat. Beat egg yolks with cream and gradually add to broth, beating with whisk. Heat, stirring, until smooth and slightly thickened. Add lemon juice and chill thoroughly. Put in chilled small serving bowls and sprinkle with cucumber, and coconut, if desired. Makes 4 servings.

SANDWICHES

John Montagu, the 4th Earl of Sandwich, was "given to eating informally at the gaming table"—and thus the sandwich was born. Today its bicentennial is being celebrated in every lunchbox and at every picnic. We salute it as a main dish, such as a club sandwich; we feature it in daintier form such as minced chicken sandwiches at receptions, teas and cocktail parties; and as a late night supper, we pay tribute to the Earl with a sliced chicken and cheese sandwich.

*Tasty Minced Chicken Sandwiches

> 1½ cups minced cooked chicken
> 1 teaspoon grated onion
> 2 tablespoons minced celery
> ½ teaspoon tarragon
> 2 tablespoons chicken broth *or* gravy
> 1 tablespoon lemon juice
> ¼ cup mayonnaise
> 2 tablespoons soft butter
> 12 slices white bread

Combine the first 3 ingredients; stir tarragon, broth and lemon juice into the mayonnaise and fold into the chicken. Adjust seasoning. Spread 6 slices of bread with butter and spread the chicken mixture on. Top with remaining bread. Cut in halves. Makes 6 sandwiches.

*Minced Chicken Sandwich Variations

To 1½ cups minced chicken mixed with ¼ cup seasoned mayonnaise add:

   ½ cup minced ham, 1 tablespoon prepared mustard
   4 slices crisp bacon, crumbled
   1 teaspoon minced onion, 1 tablespoon minced celery
      and 1 teaspoon curry powder
   ½ cup coarsely chopped water chestnuts or bean-
      sprouts, and 1 to 2 tablespoons soy sauce
   ½ cup minced smoked tongue, 1 tablespoon horseradish
   ½ cup chopped chicken livers, 1 teaspoon minced onion
      and ⅛ teaspoon oregano

Each recipe makes 4 to 6 sandwiches.

*Chicken Salad Sandwiches

   1½ cups diced cooked chicken
   ¼ cup diced celery
   ¼ cup mayonnaise
   1 tablespoon heavy cream
   ½ to 1 teaspoon salt
   2 tablespoons soft butter
   8 slices white bread

Combine the chicken and celery with mayonnaise mixed with cream and salt. Taste for seasoning. Butter 4 slices of bread and spread chicken on. Top with remaining bread and press firmly in place. Cut off crusts, if you wish. Cut in half. Makes 4 sandwiches.

*Elegant Chicken Sandwiches

Rye bread
Soft butter
Cold slices of cooked chicken
Lettuce
Sliced tomatoes
Hard-cooked eggs, sliced
Mayonnaise

For each sandwich, spread 2 slices of rye bread with butter. Arrange chicken, lettuce, tomatoes and eggs on both slices of bread. Top with mayonnaise. Serve open-faced with knives and forks.

*Chicken Club Sandwiches

12 slices buttered toast
   Sliced chicken
   Salt and pepper
2 to 4 tablespoons mayonnaise
2 tomatoes, sliced
   Small lettuce leaves
8 pieces cooked crisp bacon, cut in half

Cover 4 pieces of toast with chicken, sprinkle lightly with salt and pepper, and cover with 4 pieces of toast spread with mayonnaise. Add slices of tomato, lettuce and 4 half-slices of bacon to each sandwich. Top with the last pieces of toast. Pat down and put toothpicks on 4 sides to hold firmly in place. Cut diagonally both ways. Makes 4 sandwiches.

*Open Chicken Sandwiches

Thin slices of cooked chicken
White bread
Soft butter
Mayonnaise (optional)
Pâté (optional)

The best party sandwiches are sliced chicken ones. The number
you make depends on how much chicken you have. Spread the
bread with butter, adding a little mayonnaise to the butter if you
wish. Make them at the last minute, so they are not dry. The
most elegant sandwiches have a thin layer of pâté de foie gras
under the chicken.

*Chicken-Salad Sandwich Filling

1 can (5 ounces) boned chicken, diced, or
  ¾ cup diced cooked chicken
½ cup finely diced celery
1 tablespoon mayonnaise
1 tablespoon minced onion
1 teaspoon lemon juice
  Dash of pepper

Mix all ingredients together and use as filling for any desired
bread. Makes about 1⅓ cups.

Chopped Chicken-Liver Sandwiches

> 8 ounces chicken livers
> 3 tablespoons chicken fat *or* oil
> 1 small onion, minced
> 2 hard-cooked eggs
> 1 teaspoon minced parsley
> Salt and pepper to taste
> 4 bagels, split, toasted and buttered, *or* sliced
>   pumpernickel bread

Sauté livers in fat in skillet until lightly browned. Add onion and cook and stir over medium heat until tender. Remove livers from skillet to chopping board, add eggs and chop fine—or mash with fork in mixing bowl. Stir in parsley and season with salt and pepper. Spread thickly on bagels or bread. Makes 4 servings.

*Hot Chicken Sandwiches

> ⅓ cup flour
> 1 can (10½ ounces) cream of mushroom soup
> ¾ cup milk
> ½ teaspoon Worcestershire sauce
> 2 cups finely diced cooked chicken
> 1 teaspoon instant minced onion
> Canned pimientos
> 12 slices firm-type bread, trimmed
> 2 eggs
> ¼ cup milk
> 1 package (4½ ounces) potato chips, coarsely
>   crushed (2 cups)
> 3 tablespoons slivered blanched almonds

Put flour and soup in heavy saucepan and mix well. Add milk and bring to boil, stirring. Add Worcestershire, chicken, onion and 1 chopped pimiento. Spread in 8″ square pan and chill well.

Cut in 6 portions and put a portion on each of 6 slices bread. Top with remaining slices. Beat eggs with milk. Dip sandwiches in the mixture, then in potato chips. Put on greased baking sheet and sprinkle with almonds. Bake at 350° about 30 minutes. Garnish with pimiento strips.

*Hot Swiss-Chicken Sandwiches

Sliced cooked chicken
Sliced Swiss cheese
Bread
Eggs
Milk
Butter *or* margarine

For each sandwich, arrange chicken and cheese slices between 2 slices bread. Beat 1 egg and 1 tablespoon milk in flat dish and dip each sandwich in the mixture. Sauté in melted butter in skillet until sandwich is browned on both sides and cheese is melted.

*Top-Hat Chicken Sandwiches

6 slices toast
12 thin slices cooked chicken
1 can (14½ ounces) asparagus spears, well drained
2 tablespoons flour
1 teaspoon prepared mustard
½ teaspoon dill weed
½ teaspoon salt
Dash of pepper
1 cup evaporated skimmed milk
3 eggs, separated
½ teaspoon cream of tartar

Arrange toast on cookie sheet and top with chicken and asparagus. In saucepan, mix flour and seasonings. Gradually add milk and cook, stirring, until thickened. Remove from heat. Beat egg yolks slightly and stir into mixture. Beat egg whites and cream of tartar until stiff and fold into mixture. Spoon on asparagus and chicken. Bake at 350° about 30 minutes. Makes 6 servings.

Chicken-Cutlet Sandwiches

>   Butter
> 6 enriched sesame hamburger rolls, split and toasted
> 6 chicken cutlets (2½ ounces *each*), flattened
> 2 eggs, beaten
> ½ cup fine dry bread crumbs
> 6 lettuce leaves
>   Special Sauce (optional; see below)

Butter rolls. Dip each cutlet in egg, then in crumbs. Brown on both sides in butter and cook until done. Arrange 2 roll halves on plate, cover with lettuce leaf, then top with cutlet dipped in sauce. Spoon sauce over each sandwich. Makes 6 sandwiches.

Special Sauce

> 1 cup plus 2 tablespoons water
> ¼ cup soy sauce
> ½ cup sugar
> ½ cup chopped green pepper
> ¼ cup chopped pimiento
> 1 tablespoon white vinegar
> 2 tablespoons cornstarch

In saucepan, combine 1 cup water and next 5 ingredients. Blend cornstarch and remaining water; stir into sauce. Cook, stirring, 5 minutes, or until thickened.

*Baked Broccoli and Chicken Sandwiches

1 loaf (7 ounces) Italian or French bread
Mayonnaise
¾ pound fresh *or* 1 package (10 ounces) frozen
broccoli, cut in 3-inch pieces, cooked and
well drained
¾ pound sliced cooked chicken
⅔ cup packed coarsely shredded Cheddar cheese
2 tablespoons chicken broth

Split bread lengthwise and place cut side up on cookie sheet. Cut each in 4 diagonal pieces; spread with mayonnaise. Arrange broccoli on bottom pieces and chicken on top pieces. Stir together ½ cup mayonnaise, the cheese and broth until well blended. Spoon or spread over broccoli and chicken. Bake in preheated 425° oven until bubbly and golden brown. Makes 4 servings.

SALADS

Salads may be served first, last, in the middle of the meal, or *as* the meal; hot or cold chicken salads, the many variations of the chicken salad with vegetables or fruits, and chicken platters take the center of the stage. In fact, your skillful arrangement of colors and forms may cause your admiring guests to insist that it looks too good to eat, but with their first sampling of the flavors and textures, they will agree that the cook has taken precedence over the artist.

A great many seasonings are appropriate with chicken salads, so you may experiment—but cautiously—with tarragon, curry, capers, marjoram, rosemary, fennel, poppy seeds, chives, parsley or blended salad herbs. If using mayonnaise thin it with a little chicken gravy or concentrated chicken broth for added flavor.

*Chicken Salad

> 2 cups diced cooked chicken
> 1 cup diced celery
> ½ teaspoon salt
>   Dash of pepper
> ½ cup mayonnaise
>   Lettuce *or* other salad greens
>   Wedges of hard-cooked egg, olives, sliced
>   cucumber, tomato wedges (garnishes)

Mix first 5 ingredients and serve on salad greens, adding garnishes as desired. Makes 4 servings.

*Hot Chicken Salad

> ½ teaspoon oregano
> 1 teaspoon salt
> ¼ teaspoon pepper
> 2 cloves garlic, crushed
> ¼ cup lemon juice
> ½ cup olive oil
> 4 cups cut-up cooked chicken
> 6 new potatoes, boiled and cut in quarters
>   Water
>   Watercress *or* cut-up salad greens

Combine the oregano, salt, pepper, garlic, lemon juice and oil and heat. Warm the chicken and potatoes in a little water, add the hot dressing and stir to coat on all sides. Serve on a bed of watercress or other greens. Makes 6 servings.

*Baked Chicken Salad

  4 cups diced cooked chicken
  ¾ cup mayonnaise
  ¾ cup canned cream of chicken soup
  2 cups chopped celery
  4 hard-cooked eggs, sliced
  1 teaspoon salt
  1 teaspoon finely minced onion
  2 tablespoons lemon juice
  2 pimientos, cut up
  1 cup crushed potato chips
  ⅔ cup finely shredded sharp Cheddar cheese
  ⅓ cup chopped almonds (optional)

Mix first 9 ingredients. Put in large shallow 1½-quart baking dish.
Combine potato chips with cheese, and almonds, if used, and
sprinkle on top. Chill several hours or overnight. Bake at 400°
25 minutes, or until heated. Makes 8 servings.

*Garden Chicken Salad

  ½ cup salad oil
  ¼ cup red-wine vinegar
  ⅛ teaspoon garlic powder
  1 tablespoon chopped chives
  ½ teaspoon salt
  ⅛ teaspoon pepper
  1 teaspoon sugar
  1 package (10 ounces) fresh spinach
  3 cups diced cooked chicken
  ¾ cup chopped walnuts
  2 apples, cored and chopped

Mix first 7 ingredients and chill. Wash spinach, drain and discard
stems. Tear spinach in bite-size pieces and add chicken, walnuts
and apples. Add dressing and toss lightly. Makes 6 servings.

*Easy Chicken Salad

    3 cups diced cooked chicken
    ½ cup finely chopped celery
    ¼ cup French dressing
    ¼ cup mayonnaise
    ⅛ teaspoon cayenne
       Salad greens
       Tomato wedges

Toss together first 5 ingredients and serve on greens with a garnish of tomato wedges. Makes 4 servings.

*Chicken-Avocado Salad

    2 cups finely chopped cooked chicken
    ½ cup finely chopped celery
       Salt and pepper
    1 tablespoon lemon juice
       Dash of hot pepper sauce
    ½ cup mayonnaise
    2 large ripe avocados
    2 hard-cooked eggs, sliced

Combine all ingredients, except last 2, and mix well. Halve avocados and remove seeds. Scoop out pulp and reserve shells. Dice pulp and add to chicken mixture. Toss lightly and fill shells with the mixture. Top with egg slices. Makes 4 servings.

*Chicken-Artichoke Salad

        2 cups diced cooked chicken
        1 can (15 ounces) artichoke hearts, drained
        ¼ cup heavy cream
        ½ cup mayonnaise
        2 tablespoons catsup
           Dash of Worcestershire sauce
           Salt and pepper
        ¼ cup chopped pitted black olives
           Lettuce

Combine first 2 ingredients in bowl and chill. Whip cream and
mix with next 3 ingredients, and salt and pepper to taste. Add
olives and chill. When ready to serve, fold dressing into chicken
mixture and arrange on lettuce in serving bowl. Makes 4 to 6
servings.

*Pineapple Chicken Salad

        2 cups diced cold cooked chicken
        1 can (8 ounces) pineapple, diced
        1 cup diced celery
        1 apple, cored and chopped
        ⅔ cup raisins
           Mayonnaise to moisten
           Salt and pepper to taste
           Salad greens

Combine all ingredients, except greens. Toss and chill. Serve on
greens. Makes 6 servings.

*Chicken-Grape Salad

> 2 cups diced cooked chicken
> 1 cup sliced celery
> ¼ cup French dressing
> 2 cups seedless grapes, halved if large
> Salt and pepper
> Salad greens
> ¼ cup *each* mayonnaise and sour cream

Marinate chicken and celery in the French dressing 1 hour. Add grapes and season to taste with salt and pepper. Arrange on greens. Mix mayonnaise and sour cream and top salad with the mixture. Makes 6 servings.

*Chicken Salad with Oranges

> 4 cups bite-size pieces of cooked chicken
> 2 oranges, sectioned
> ¼ cup grated coconut
> 1 package (3 ounces) cream cheese
> ¼ cup heavy cream
> ¼ cup orange juice
> Few drops lemon juice
> 1 teaspoon salt
> 1 teaspoon curry powder

Combine the chicken with orange sections and coconut in a bowl. Blend the cheese and cream with orange and lemon juices, salt and curry. Pour over the chicken and stir gently but thoroughly. Makes 6 servings.

*Chicken Salad with Pineapple

    2½ cups diced cooked chicken
     2 cups coarsely chopped celery
     2 cups fresh pineapple chunks *or* 1 can (20 ounces)
        pineapple tidbits, drained
    ½ cup mayonnaise
    ½ teaspoon salt
      Pepper to taste
      Salad greens
    ½ cup chopped walnuts (optional)

In large bowl combine chicken, celery, pineapple chunks, mayonnaise, salt and pepper. Arrange greens in salad bowl and top with chicken mixture. Sprinkle with walnuts. Makes 6 servings.

*Curried Chicken-Rice Salad

    ½ cup mayonnaise
     1 tablespoon milk
     1 teaspoon lemon juice
    ½ teaspoon curry powder
    ⅛ teaspoon salt
     3 cups chopped cooked chicken
    ½ cup thinly sliced celery
     1 cup cooked rice
     2 tablespoons chopped pimiento

Mix together until well blended mayonnaise, milk, lemon juice, curry powder and salt. Add chicken and celery and mix well. Mix together rice and pimiento. Layer chicken salad and the rice mixture in a glass serving dish. Makes 6 servings.

*Chicken-Rice Salad

1 cup raw rice
2 cups chicken broth
2 cups diced cooked chicken
2 cups finely chopped celery
1 tablespoon finely minced onion
1 cup mayonnaise
¼ cup lemon juice
1 teaspoon salt
¼ teaspoon pepper
Paprika

Cook rice in chicken broth. Cool. Add chicken, celery and onion. Mix next 4 ingredients, add to rice mixture and toss until well mixed. Chill. Sprinkle with paprika. Makes 6 servings.

*Oriental Chicken Salad

3 cups diced cooked chicken
1 can (13¼ ounces) pineapple tidbits, drained
2 tablespoons sliced green onion
1 can (6 ounces) water chestnuts, drained and slivered
6 tablespoons *each* mayonnaise and dairy sour cream
½ teaspoon *each* salt and ground ginger
⅛ teaspoon pepper
¼ cup toasted slivered almonds
Salad greens

Combine first 4 ingredients and chill. Mix remaining ingredients, except almonds and greens, and add to chicken mixture. Toss lightly, then sprinkle with almonds. Serve on greens. Makes 4 to 6 servings.

Chicken-Walnut-Orange Salad

2 chicken breasts, boned and cut in 1-inch pieces
Oil
Pinch of nutmeg
6 cups torn assorted salad greens (romaine, Boston,
    Bibb, iceberg *and/or* escarole)
3 oranges, peeled and sliced
½ cup chopped walnuts
⅓ cup orange juice
1 teaspoon salt
Pepper to taste

Sauté chicken in 1 tablespoon oil until lightly browned and tender; sprinkle with nutmeg. Chill. Toss chicken, greens, oranges, walnuts, orange juice, ¼ cup oil, salt and pepper. Makes 4 servings.

*Chicken in Aspic

3 envelopes unflavored gelatin
3 cups chicken broth
½ cup white wine
Fresh tarragon leaves if available
6 slices boiled ham
3 cups diced cooked chicken
Salad greens

Sprinkle the gelatin on the broth and heat until gelatin is dissolved, 2 or 3 minutes. Add the wine. Use 6 individual molds that hold at least a cup (or use a 2-quart mold or dish). Place crossed pieces of tarragon in the bottom of each serving. Pour in a little gelatin and cool until set. Add ham slices cut to fit and fill with chicken. Add remaining gelatin and chill 3 or 4 hours, until set. Turn out on greens. Makes 6 servings.

*Tangy Chicken Mold

        2 envelopes unflavored gelatin
        1 can (12 ounces) beer
    1½ cups well-seasoned chicken broth
        1 teaspoon sugar
        1 teaspoon instant minced onion
        2 cups diced cooked chicken
        1 cup cooked peas
        ½ cup diced celery
          Salt and white pepper to taste
          Lettuce *or* other salad greens
          Curry mayonnaise *or* green-goddess dressing

Soften gelatin in ½ cup beer. Heat ½ cup chicken broth, add to gelatin and stir until dissolved. Add remaining broth and beer and next 2 ingredients. Chill until thickened but not firm. Fold in next 3 ingredients and season with salt and pepper to taste. Pour into 5-cup ring mold and chill until firm. Turn out on bed of lettuce and top with dressing. Makes 6 servings.

Hot Chicken Mousse

        3 cups ground raw chicken
        ½ teaspoon salt
        ¼ teaspoon paprika
        ¼ teaspoon celery salt
        1 cup heavy cream
        4 egg whites, beaten stiff
          Canned pimiento strips

Combine the chicken with the next 4 ingredients and stir into a paste. Fold in the egg whites. Line a mold or 6 custard cups with pimiento and pour in the chicken mixture. Do not fill more than ¾ full. Bake at 325° for 40 minutes for a large mold, 35 minutes for small. Turn out. Serves 6.

*Lemon Chicken Mousse

    1 package (3 ounces) lemon-flavored gelatin, softened
      Water
    2 tablespoons lemon juice
    ½ cup chopped green pepper
    1 canned pimiento, chopped
    3 cups minced cooked chicken
      Salad greens

Dissolve the gelatin in 1 cup boiling water, add ½ cup cold water and the lemon juice. Chill until slightly thickened. Mix the green pepper, pimiento and chicken and add to the gelatin. Mix and pour into a 5-cup mold. Chill until firm. Serve on greens. Makes 4 to 6 servings.

*Chicken, Fruit and Bean Plate

    4 to 8 slices cold cooked chicken
    4 plums, halved
    4 peaches, halved
    2 cups drained cooked green beans
    3 tablespoons mayonnaise
      Grated orange rind
      French dressing
    1 teaspoon sugar
    2 tablespoons orange juice

On each of 4 chilled plates arrange the chicken slices. Place the plums and peaches, fresh or canned, on the side of the plate and put the beans in a pile. Dab the mayonnaise on the chicken and put the orange rind on the beans. Sprinkle with a little French dressing mixed with the sugar and orange juice. Makes 4 servings.

*Cold Chicken Plate

    8 slices cooked chicken
    2 tablespoons minced parsley
    1 can (16 ounces) apricots, plums *or* peaches
    1 package (10 ounces) frozen peas, cooked
        according to directions
    Chopped mint
    1 cup mayonnaise

Place 2 slices of chicken on each of 4 cold plates and sprinkle with parsley. Place the fruit on one side of the plate and the chilled peas on the other. Sprinkle the peas with mint. Dot chicken and peas with mayonnaise. Pass remaining mayonnaise. Makes 4 servings.

PART V

Leftovers

17 *Leftovers*

*An asterisk (*) is placed before all recipes
that are made from chicken
which has been previously cooked.*

Leftovers have come a long way since the days when they evoked
loud groans in boardinghouses throughout the land. Who could
complain about such dishes as Chicken Tetrazzini or Chicken
Divan, both of which must be made from cooked chicken. In a
sense, we do distinguish between true leftovers of the "What-
shall-I-do-with-the-chicken-they-didn't-eat?" variety and the extra fowl we cooked on Thursday in order to have chicken salad
with white grapes on Sunday evening. But both the true and the
planned leftover are invaluable, and the former provides even
more of a challenge than the latter.

Small amounts of leftover broiler-fryers, fowl or roasted
chicken can be whirled in a blender with a little broth or other
liquid, and used to thicken and flavor soups, stews and gravies. A
little chicken puree does wonders for salad dressings and sauces.
Chicken ground with other good things such as celery and onions
makes a splendid stuffing for baked potatoes, green peppers, tomatoes and hard-cooked eggs. Chopped chicken with mayonnaise
and herbs serves as a canapé, dip or spread and, with the addition of a little minced ham or crumbled crisp bacon, becomes
a tasty sandwich spread. Minced cooked chicken is required for

chicken soufflé and for croquettes. Stir some into scrambled eggs; or add a cream sauce and you have a filling for omelets, pancakes or patty shells. Bits of chicken provide taste and texture in a risotto or a pasta sauce.

Planned leftovers include all recipes calling for "previously cooked" chicken. Although cookbooks used to say "boiled fowl" or "poached broilers" when describing the cut-up meat in a specific dish, this actually makes little, if any, difference. It is true that a large bird will provide handsome slices of breast for a Chicken Divan, but the sauce will cover a multitude of smaller pieces very nicely. With ingenuity and imagination, one can plan for two quite dissimilar meals and do most of the cooking for both at the same time. It isn't even necessary to make definite plans: for example, the meat of an extra bird, roasted or fricasseed, can be frozen for some future use, and so can the broth made from its bones.

Of course there is nothing wrong with the old-fashioned "warmed-over" dish—in the case of a casserole, it can be better than the original. And if one has a favorite or party specialty, doubling the quantity will guarantee a subsequent treat ready in the freezer. The cook who knows her leftovers will have time left over for other things and, in addition, will save plenty of energy—her own and the utility company's.

*Chicken Pâté

> 2 cups ground cooked chicken
> 2 hard-cooked eggs, chopped fine
> Dash of hot pepper sauce
> 1 teaspoon Worcestershire sauce
> 1 teaspoon salt
> ½ cup ground almonds *or* other nuts
> Wine *or* brandy

Combine all the ingredients, using enough wine or brandy to make proper consistency to spread. Makes 8 canapé servings.

*Chicken Newburg

      3 tablespoons butter
      3 tablespoons flour
     ½ cup chicken broth
      3 to 3½ cups diced cooked chicken
     ½ teaspoon salt
      2 egg yolks
     ½ cup heavy cream *or* half-and-half
     ¼ cup sherry
      1 to 2 tablespoons brandy
        Dash nutmeg
        Toast, rice *or* waffles

Melt the butter and blend in the flour; do *not* let brown. Pour in the broth slowly while stirring. Add the chicken and salt. Combine the egg yolks with cream and sherry and stir in. Continue to heat, stirring constantly, while adding the brandy and nutmeg. Serve over toast, rice or waffles. Makes 4 to 6 servings.

*Chicken Newburg with Grapes

     ¼ cup butter
      2 cups diced cooked chicken
      4 tablespoons sherry
    1½ cups half-and-half
      4 egg yolks
     ¾ cup drained canned seedless grapes
     ¼ cup flaked coconut
        Seasoned salt
        White pepper
        Hot toast, rice *or* patty shells
        Paprika

Heat butter, chicken, 2 tablespoons sherry and the half-and-half in top part of double boiler over simmering water. Beat remaining sherry with the egg yolks. Add small amount of hot mixture, stirring. Put back in double boiler and cook, stirring, until thickened. Add grapes and coconut and season to taste. Serve on toast with a sprinkling of paprika. Makes 4 servings.

*Chicken à la King

        1 green pepper, chopped
        2 tablespoons butter
        1 cup sliced mushrooms *or* 1 can (4 ounces), drained
        1 pimiento, chopped
        3 tablespoons flour
        2 cups half-and-half
    2½ to 3 cups diced cooked chicken
        1 teaspoon salt
      ¼ teaspoon pepper
        2 egg yolks, beaten
        3 tablespoons sherry
          Patty shells, toast *or* rice

Sauté the green pepper in butter for 4 or 5 minutes; add mushrooms and sauté 3 minutes; add the pimiento. Blend in the flour and pour in the half-and-half slowly while stirring. Add the chicken, salt and pepper and bring to a boil for 2 minutes. Combine the egg yolks with sherry, add and cook gently for 2 minutes. Serve in patty shells, on toast or with rice. Makes 6 servings.

*Chicken Divan

> 1 bunch broccoli *or* 2 packages (10 ounces
>   *each*) frozen
> Salt
> Water
> ¼ cup butter
> ¼ cup flour
> 1½ cups half-and-half
> ½ cup chicken broth
>   Pepper
> 1 cup grated Parmesan cheese
>   Slices of poached *or* roasted chicken breast

Wash the broccoli and, if using fresh, scrape the stems. Cook
in salted water until tender. If using frozen, follow package instructions. Meanwhile make the sauce. Melt the butter, stir in
the flour; do not brown. Pour in the half-and-half and broth
slowly while stirring. Add salt and pepper to taste, cook until
smooth and thickened, and add ½ cup of Parmesan cheese; stir
and cook until the cheese melts. Place the broccoli in a shallow
oven-proof dish and put the chicken slices over it. Pour on the
cream sauce and sprinkle remaining cheese on top. Heat under
the broiler, not too close to the heat, until the sauce is bubbly
and cheese lightly browned. Makes 6 servings.

*Chicken Tetrazzini

> 1 package (8 ounces) thin spaghetti
> 2 cans (13½ ounces *each*) chicken broth
> 1 pound mushrooms, sliced
> 1 clove garlic, crushed
> ¼ cup butter
> 3 tablespoons flour
> ½ cup heavy cream *or* half-and-half
> 3 cups cooked chicken, diced
> ⅓ cup grated Parmesan cheese

Boil the spaghetti in the broth for about 5 minutes, until barely tender. Drain, reserving broth. Boil the broth to reduce it to about 2 cups. Meanwhile, brown the mushrooms and garlic in 2 tablespoons butter, remove and set aside. Add remaining butter and blend in the flour. Slowly stir in the chicken broth and the cream. Cook and stir until smooth and thickened. Put ⅓ of the spaghetti in a large casserole, cover with 1 cup of chicken, a layer of mushrooms and ⅓ of the cream sauce. Sprinkle with a little cheese. Repeat twice more, ending with cream sauce on top. Sprinkle with remaining cheese. Bake at 450° until bubbly and brown on top. Makes 6 servings.

*Chicken Hash I

- 2 cups diced cooked chicken
- 1 cup boiled potatoes, diced
- 1 cup leftover chicken gravy *or* strong broth
- 1 tablespoon minced scallions *or* chives
- 1 tablespoon minced parsley
- 1 tablespoon minced green pepper (optional)

Combine all of the ingredients and adjust seasoning. Heat gently on top of the stove, or cover and bake at 350° about 20 minutes, until heated through. Makes 4 servings.

*Chicken Hash II

- 1 large onion, finely chopped
- 2 tablespoons butter *or* margarine
- 2 cups diced cooked potatoes
- 2 cups diced cooked chicken
- 2 tablespoons minced parsley
- ½ teaspoon salt
- ¼ teaspoon pepper

Sauté the onion in butter until light brown. Add remaining ingredients and stir. Flatten on top and cook for about 10 minutes, until brown. Put under broiler and brown the top. Turn out on a warm platter, or cook the hash in a low casserole and bring it to the table from the broiler. Makes 4 servings.

*Chicken Hash De Luxe

      1 tablespoon minced onion
      2 tablespoons butter *or* chicken fat
      2 tablespoons flour
      ½ cup chicken broth
      ½ cup milk
      1 cup cream
   2½ to 3 cups cooked diced chicken
      2 egg yolks
      ¼ cup grated Italian *or* Swiss cheese

Sauté the onion in butter until transparent. Stir in the flour and pour in the chicken broth and milk slowly while stirring. Simmer until smooth and thickened. Add ½ cup cream and the chicken and heat. Add salt and pepper to taste. Pour into a casserole. Beat the egg yolks with remaining cream and mix in the cheese. Pour over the hash and heat in 400° oven until bubbly, about 25 minutes. Makes 4 servings.

*Baked Chicken Hash

      1 tablespoon butter
      1 tablespoon chicken fat
   1½ tablespoons flour
      1 cup chicken broth
         Salt and pepper
   2½ cups finely diced cooked chicken

Melt the butter and chicken fat together. Blend in the flour and stir in the chicken broth. Add salt and pepper to taste—the amount will depend upon the seasoning in the broth. When smooth and thickened, add the chicken and pour into a baking dish. Bake at 350° for 20 minutes. Makes 4 servings.

*Chicken Hash with Vegetables

    2½ cups diced cooked chicken
    ½ cup cooked diced celery
    ½ cup cooked diced onions
    ½ cup cooked diced potatoes
    1 cup chicken gravy *or* strong broth
    ½ cup tomato puree
      Salt and pepper
    ½ teaspoon poultry seasoning
    2 tablespoons butter *or* chicken fat

Combine all of the ingredients except the butter. Blend thoroughly and put into a baking dish. Dot with butter and bake at 350° for 20 to 30 minutes, until heated through and slightly brown on top. Makes 4 to 6 servings.

*Chicken Croquettes I

    6 tablespoons flour
    6 tablespoons butter
    2 teaspoons salt
    ¼ teaspoon pepper
    2 cups milk
    2 tablespoons minced onion
    3 cups diced cooked chicken
    2 cups cracker crumbs
    1 egg beaten with 1 tablespoon water
      Fat for deep frying

Blend the flour into melted butter. Add salt and pepper and pour in the milk slowly, stirring constantly. Simmer until thick and smooth. Blend in the onion and chicken and chill several hours or longer. Shape into about 9 croquettes. Roll them in the cracker crumbs, then in the egg beaten with water, then in the crumbs again. Fry in deep fat at 365° until light brown. Good served with rice. Makes 6 servings.

*Chicken Croquettes II

    ¼ cup butter
    ⅓ cup flour
    ½ cup chicken broth
    1 cup milk
    1 teaspoon salt
    ¼ teaspoon pepper
    2 egg yolks and 1 egg
    3 cups minced chicken
    2 tablespoons minced chives *or* scallions
    2 tablespoons minced parsley
    ½ teaspoon tarragon *or* basil
    1 tablespoon water
      Fine dry bread crumbs
      Fat for deep frying

Melt the butter, smooth in the flour and pour in the broth. Simmer, thin with the milk, stirring steadily. Add salt and pepper and the egg yolks, mixing thoroughly. Stir in the chicken, chives, parsley and tarragon; form into shapes about 2½" to 3" long and as thick as your thumb. Mix the whole egg with the water; roll the croquettes in this and then in bread crumbs. Fry in deep fat at 375° until golden brown. Makes 6 servings.

*Chicken Croquettes with Curry and Lemon

     ¼ cup flour
     ¼ cup butter
     ½ cup chicken broth
     ½ cup half-and-half *or* cream
     1 teaspoon salt
     ¼ teaspoon pepper
     2 cups chopped cooked chicken
     1 to 2 teaspoons curry powder
     ½ teaspoon celery salt
     1 to 2 teaspoons lemon juice
     2 teaspoons minced parsley
       Bread crumbs
     1 egg beaten with 2 tablespoons water
       Oil for deep frying

Blend the flour into the melted butter. When smooth, pour in the broth and half-and-half slowly while stirring. Add salt and pepper. Meanwhile combine the chicken with curry, celery salt, lemon juice and parsley. Mix with the sauce, using enough sauce to make a soft mixture but firm enough to hold a shape. Make into small long croquettes; dip in crumbs and egg and then coat with crumbs. Chill for a few minutes or longer and fry in vegetable oil. Makes 6 servings.

*Chicken and Rice Loaf I

    2 tablespoons flour
    2 tablespoons butter
    1 cup chicken broth
    3 cups diced cooked chicken
    1 teaspoon salt
    ¼ teaspoon pepper
    1 tablespoon minced onion
    3 tablespoons chili sauce
    1 teaspoon Worcestershire sauce
    1 teaspoon minced parsley
    2 cups cooked rice

Stir the flour into the melted butter and blend. Pour the broth in slowly while simmering and stirring. Season the chicken with salt and pepper and add remaining ingredients except the rice. Combine chicken mixture with the sauce. Spread half the rice in a greased loaf pan, spread the chicken over the rice and top with remaining rice. Press down. Set the loaf pan in a larger pan filled with hot water about ¾" deep. Bake at 350° for 45 minutes. Turn out on a warm platter. Makes 6 servings.

*Chicken and Rice Loaf II

    4 cups cooked chicken, finely ground
    1 cup cooked rice
    1 teaspoon salt
    1 teaspoon lemon juice
    ¼ cup minced parsley
    ½ cup minced celery
    ⅛ cup minced onion
    2 eggs, beaten
    1 cup chicken broth

Mix the chicken and rice, season with salt and lemon juice and stir in the parsley and vegetables. Mix the eggs into the chicken broth and pour into the chicken mixture. Blend well. Turn into a greased loaf pan and place in a larger pan filled with hot water about 1″ deep. Bake at 350° for 45 minutes. Turn out on a warm serving plate. Makes 6 servings.

*Macaroni and Cheese with Chicken

> 1 package macaroni with cheese sauce
> 1 to 2 cups diced cooked chicken
> 1 cup any leftover cooked vegetable, such as peas, beans or carrots

Prepare the macaroni as directed. Add the cut-up chicken and any vegetables and reheat. Makes 4 servings.

*Baked Chicken-Rice Custard

> 4 eggs
> 1½ cups milk
> ½ cup chopped green pepper
> 1 teaspoon salt
> ½ teaspoon poultry seasoning
> ¼ teaspoon pepper
> 1 can (13½ ounces) fried rice with chicken
> 1 cup chopped cooked chicken

Beat eggs slightly and add next 5 ingredients. Stir in rice, separating with fork, and the chopped chicken. Bake in greased shallow 1½-quart baking dish set in pan of hot water at 325° 1 hour, or until set. Cut in squares. Serves 4 to 6.

*Chicken Pilaf

> 1 cup chopped onion
> ½ cup chopped celery
> 2 tablespoons butter *or* margarine
> 1 cup raw rice
> ½ teaspoon thyme
> 1 can (13 ounces) boned chicken with broth *or*
>   1 pound cooked chicken
> 2 cups chicken broth
> ¾ cup chopped walnuts

In large heavy saucepan or Dutch oven, sauté onion and celery in the butter until onion is golden. Add rice and thyme and continue to cook, stirring, until rice is golden. Cut chicken in bite-size pieces and add to rice with its broth, if canned chicken is used, and the additional broth. Bring to boil, cover and simmer 20 minutes, or until rice is tender and all liquid is absorbed. Add walnuts and toss lightly. Makes 4 servings.

*Chicken-Ham Mousse

> 1 cup chicken broth
> 1 cup milk
> 1 envelope unflavored gelatin
> 2 egg yolks
> 1 cup ground cooked ham
> 2 cups ground cooked chicken
> ¼ teaspoon paprika
> 1 pimiento, chopped
> 1 cup heavy cream
>   Salt and pepper
> 2 tablespoons minced parsley

Put broth and milk in a double boiler; sprinkle gelatin on liquids. Beat in egg yolks. Cook, stirring constantly, until mixture is slightly thickened. Put the mixture in a large bowl and cool. Add ham, chicken, paprika, pimiento, cream and salt and pepper to taste. Pour into 3½-cup loaf pan and chill until firm. Turn out and garnish with minced parsley. Makes 6 servings.

*Risi Bisi

        1 medium onion, minced
        ¼ cup butter
        ½ cup shredded ham
        3 cups chicken broth
     1½ cups raw rice
        2 cups minced cooked chicken
        ¼ cup grated Parmesan cheese

Sauté the onion gently in 2 tablespoons butter until golden. Add the next 4 ingredients. Simmer for about 25 minutes, until the rice is dry but not too soft and the liquid absorbed. Stir in the remaining butter and the cheese. Makes 6 servings.

*Chicken and Noodles

        3 tablespoons butter
        3 tablespoons flour
        1 teaspoon salt
        ¼ teaspoon pepper
     1½ cups milk
        3 cups diced cooked chicken
        1 package (8 ounces) noodles, cooked
        1 tablespoon minced chives *or* scallions
        1 tablespoon minced parsley
        ½ cup grated Italian cheese

Melt the butter over low heat, blend in the flour, add the salt and pepper and then pour in the milk slowly while stirring. Stir and cook until smooth and thickened. Add the chicken and heat. Place the hot noodles in a casserole or oven-proof dish; stir in the chives, parsley and ¼ cup cheese. Pour the chicken and sauce over the noodles. Mix and top with remaining cheese. Place under broiler until hot and bubbly and the cheese melts and browns. Makes 6 servings.

*Chicken Pyramid

    1 can (4 ounces) mushroom stems and pieces, drained
    3 cups ground or chopped cooked chicken
    1 cup cream of chicken soup
    2 cups mashed potatoes
    4 tablespoons grated Cheddar or other cheese
      Melted butter or margarine
    ¼ cup soft bread crumbs

Mix first 3 ingredients and shape in pyramid in greased shallow baking dish. Cover with mixture of potatoes and 2 tablespoons cheese. Pour a little melted butter over top and sprinkle with crumbs mixed with remaining cheese. Bake at 425° about 20 minutes. Makes 4 to 6 servings.

*One-Dish Chicken Dinner

> 4 cups thinly sliced peeled potatoes
> Salt and pepper
> 3 cups cubed cooked chicken
> 1 package (10 ounces) frozen green peas,
>   partially thawed
> 1 can (10½ ounces) cream of chicken soup
> ½ soup-can milk
> 2 tablespoons instant minced onion
> 1 teaspoon Worcestershire sauce
> ½ teaspoon marjoram
> ¼ teaspoon dry mustard
> ⅛ teaspoon pepper
>   Dash of hot pepper sauce
>   Paprika

Arrange half the potatoes in 11½" x 7½" x 1½" baking dish. Sprinkle with salt and pepper. Top with the chicken, peas and remaining potatoes. Sprinkle with salt and pepper. In saucepan, combine remaining ingredients, except paprika, and heat through. Pour evenly over potato mixture. Cover and bake in preheated 375° oven 1 hour. Sprinkle with paprika. Makes 6 servings.

*Eggplant Stuffed with Leftover Chicken

> 1 large eggplant
> 4 tablespoons chopped onion
> ¼ cup oil, part olive
> 2 tomatoes, peeled and chopped
> 2 cups cooked chicken, cut up
> 1 teaspoon salt
> ¼ teaspoon pepper
>   Pinch oregano
> 2 tablespoons chopped parsley

Parboil the eggplant 10 minutes. Cut in half lengthwise and scoop out pulp. Brown onion in 2 tablespoons oil; add tomatoes and eggplant pulp and cook a few more minutes. Add the chicken, salt, pepper and oregano. Stuff the eggplant; sprinkle with remaining oil and chopped parsley. Bake at 350° for 20 minutes. Makes 4 servings.

*Cold Spinach Roll with Chicken Mayonnaise

> 3 pounds fresh spinach *or* 3 packages (10 ounces *each*) frozen chopped spinach
> 9 tablespoons butter
> Salt, pepper and nutmeg
> 4 eggs, separated
> ½ cup fine dry bread crumbs
> 4 or more tablespoons grated Parmesan cheese
> 2 cups diced cold cooked chicken
> ½ cup thinly sliced radishes
> ⅓ cup toasted almonds
> 2 tablespoons chopped parsley
> Mayonnaise

If using fresh spinach, wash well in lukewarm water and remove stems. Place in large saucepan without any water except that clinging to the leaves, cover tightly and wilt down over medium heat. Drain well and chop coarsely. If using frozen spinach, thaw over low heat, then squeeze out moisture with hands. Put spinach in bowl and mix with 6 tablespoons melted butter and salt, pepper and nutmeg to taste. Beat in egg yolks one at a time. Line a 15″ x 10″ x 1″ jelly-roll pan with heavy waxed paper and butter well with remaining butter. Sprinkle with the bread crumbs. Beat egg whites until they hold soft peaks, then fold into spinach mixture. At once turn into prepared pan and spread evenly with rubber spatula. Sprinkle top with Parmesan. Put into preheated 350° oven and bake about 15 minutes, or until center feels barely firm when lightly touched with fingertip. Remove from oven and cool thoroughly. Spread cooled roll with chicken mayonnaise made by mixing next 4 ingredients with enough mayonnaise to bind (about ½ cup). Roll up carefully from long side. Put on platter and slice to serve. Makes 6 servings.

*Tomatoes Stuffed with Chicken Hash

        6 large tomatoes
        2 tablespoons butter *or* margarine
        ¼ cup finely chopped onion
        1 tablespoon flour
        ½ cup milk *or* chicken broth
        2 teaspoons Worcestershire sauce
        2 cups finely diced cooked chicken
        ½ cup diced cooked potatoes
           Salt and pepper

Cut a slice off top of each tomato and scoop out pulp. Melt butter, add onion and cook until tender. Stir in flour, then add milk and cook, stirring, until thickened; add Worcestershire. Combine with chicken, potatoes and a little tomato pulp. Season to taste with salt and pepper and stuff tomatoes with the mixture. Bake in preheated 375° oven 25 minutes. Makes 6 servings.

Basic Omelet

        6 eggs
        ¼ teaspoon salt
        ⅛ teaspoon pepper
        2 tablespoons water *or* milk
        2 tablespoons butter

Using fork, beat the eggs, salt, pepper and water or milk together in a bowl. (Water makes a more delicate omelet.) Put the butter in a hot pan and as soon as it foams pour in the eggs. Stir imme-

diately with one hand while shaking the pan. Lift the edges of
the omelet with the fork to let the loose portions run under.
When almost set, turn off the heat, stop stirring and let the
omelet rest for 30 seconds. Fold the omelet over, using a spatula,
tilt the pan over a warm platter and turn it once more as you
slip it onto the platter. The whole process should take about 2
minutes. Makes 2 or 3 servings.

*Omelet with Chicken

    ¼ cup milk
    1 can (10½ ounces) cream of chicken soup
    ½ teaspoon salt
    1 tablespoon Worcestershire sauce
    1 cup finely diced cooked chicken
      Basic Omelet (made with 4 eggs)
      Chopped parsley

Heat all of the ingredients except the omelet and parsley. When
smooth and slightly thickened, set aside. Make the omelet and
cover half with the chicken mixture, fold over onto a warm platter and top with remaining chicken. Sprinkle with parsley and
serve at once. Makes 2 or 3 servings.

*Fluffy Omelet with Creamed Chicken

    6 eggs, separated
    6 tablespoons milk
    ½ teaspoon salt
      Dash of pepper
    2 tablespoons margarine
    1 can (10¾ ounces) chicken gravy
    1 cup diced cooked chicken
      Chopped parsley

Beat egg yolks until thick and lemon-colored. Stir in milk and seasonings. Beat egg whites until stiff, then fold in egg-yolk mixture. Melt margarine in 9" skillet and, when hot, pour in mixture. Cook over low heat 3 to 5 minutes, or until omelet is lightly browned on bottom. Put under broiler a few inches from heat and cook until omelet is set and top springs back when touched. Meanwhile, combine gravy and chicken and heat. Slide half the omelet onto platter, pour three fourths of mixture on omelet half and fold other half over. Pour remaining mixture on top and sprinkle with parsley. Makes 4 servings.

*Chicken-Filled Pancakes

        3 eggs
        1 cup flour
    ¼ teaspoon baking soda
        2 cups buttermilk
          Butter *or* margarine
        2 cups chopped cooked chicken
        1 cup finely chopped celery
        1 can (10½ ounces) cream of chicken soup
        1 cup sour cream
          Nutmeg
          Salt and pepper

Beat eggs with rotary beater. Add next 3 ingredients and beat with spoon until smooth. Heat an 8" skillet (cast-iron or coated aluminum type with sloping sides is good) and brush with melted butter. Pour about ¼ cup batter into hot pan, tilting at once so batter covers bottom and gives crisp, uneven edges. When browned on one side, turn and brown other. Remove to rack. Repeat with remaining batter. Makes 12 to 14. To make filling, combine in saucepan the chicken, celery and ½ cup each soup and sour cream. Heat gently and season with dash of nutmeg and salt and pepper to taste. Put about 3 tablespoons hot filling on each pancake, roll up and put on broiler-proof platter or pan. Combine remaining soup and sour cream and heat. Add dash of nutmeg and salt and pepper to taste and spoon dollop on each pancake. Put under broiler until heated. Makes 4 to 6 servings.

Index

H 29